BURNING BRIDGES

BURNING BRIDGES

DIARY OF A MIDLIFE AFFAIR

Inette Miller

G. P. Putnam's Sons / New York

G. P. Putnam's Sons
Publishers Since 1838
200 Madison Avenue
New York, NY 10016

Designed by Rhea Braunstein

Library of Congress Cataloging-in-Publication Data

Miller, Inette.
Burning bridges.

1. Miller, Inette—Diaries.   2. Middle aged
women—United States—Diaries.   3. Adultery—
United States—Case studies.   I. Title.
HQ1059.5.U5M55   1987   305.4   87-10847
ISBN 0-399-13320-8

Printed in the United States of America
3   4   5   6   7   8   9   10

To my sons, with love

"You are you. Just as I am me," said the wise old butterfly. "Nothing more, nothing less."

—Stephen Cosgrove,
Flutterby

We have two or three great moving experiences in our lives—experiences so great and moving that it doesn't seem at the time that anyone else has been caught up and pounded and dazzled and astonished and beaten and broken and rescued and illuminated and rewarded and humbled in just that way ever before.

—F. Scott Fitzgerald

PROLOGUE

I was born on Mother's Day, 1946—the third child and long-awaited daughter, after two sons. This is the sort of detail that is inconsequential except in the important arena of family lore. It meant my parents could stop making babies; they had their girl. It also meant, if I did nothing else original for the rest of my life, I was special—the baby, the female—and distinctive for having let out my first wail on Mother's Day. The family I was born into was Jewish and comfortably affluent.

When I was eighteen months and toddling, my next oldest brother, then five, rammed his tricycle handlebar into my mouth and knocked my two large front teeth to the sidewalk. In a family that placed an exceedingly high value on big smiles, with a mother whose great pride was being "the girl with the million-dollar smile," this incident was the stuff of family legend. My poor middle brother paid his psychic dues for the act he called unintentional. And I learned the lesson well that life with two older males was going to give me a run for my money.

At three I was entered into my first contest. I walked away with a heavy brass loving cup for having acquired the darkest tan at Carlins' Park Swimming Pool. The victory cup sat proudly in our club basement for the duration of my childhood and sits in my office now. I learned at the side of my mother that competition is what life is about—either you win or you lose.

At four, I was promised a trip to the furniture store to replace my crib with a big bed, and I was brimming with excitement. There was one catch—the trip was a fraud. The furniture store turned out to be a hospital, and I was wheeled into surgery in a state of unmitigated terror to have my tonsils removed. For months after, I had recurrent nightmares that my bed was full of snakes. From this I learned that things are not always what they seem—but I'm not sure I've yet learned that lesson well.

My childhood was easy: I was smart, responsible, and indulged. I was outgoing, verbal, and something of an athlete. I was also bossy. I studied piano and violin, elocution and modeling, tap dance and modern jazz. I had braces and contact lenses and plastic surgery on my nose when I was fifteen.

My father's childhood hadn't been so easy. He was one of nine children of Russian immigrants—very poor and forced out of school and into the marketplace far too young. He is one of that authentic breed that emerged from the depression, a self-made businessman: successful, honest, and generous to a fault. He was determined that his children would experience neither his economic nor his educational deprivation.

There was never a question that all his children would be educated. College was not an option, it was a requirement. Each of my brothers had three choices—he could study medicine, dentistry, or the law. I had three choices—I could marry a man who studied medicine, dentistry, or the law. But what else is new? These attitudes are so classic that, until I met my husband, I didn't *know* anyone who didn't share my family's values.

My mother grew up far more middle class. *Her* father owned real estate, a business of his own, and was president of the synagogue. She was in awe of her immigrant father's drive, his elegance, and his accomplishment; and repeatedly told me, "You are the child most like my father."

My mother's messages to me were double edged, even if my father's were not. "I have never *had* to work," she crowed, proud that two hard-working men had supported her for her entire life. She openly delighted that her smile, her curls, and her style had won her many beaux and innumerable proposals of marriage. And for her daughter she wanted all that, but not *only* that. I was, after all, the child most like her father: ambitious, aggressive, a risk taker. She wanted me to be able to compete in the traditional male world, and she wanted me to be attractive and appealing to a suitably rich husband. To that latter end, she spared no expense. Without exaggeration, my mother and I spent every leisure hour between my years of twelve and eighteen shopping. When I think of my rather tumultuous adolescence, I think of being locked in combat with my mother in some department store dressing room, with a pitiful saleswoman trying to referee on matters of taste. Ultimately, my mother resolved *her* conflict by telling me that I could do it all; "you *can* do whatever it is you *want* to do." It was a long time indeed, before I realized that was just not so.

Paul and I were kids when we met—just twenty. He took me out on my twenty-first birthday for my first legal drink. At the time, we were students in Florence, Italy, on our junior year of college abroad. He took me for that drink in a horse-drawn carriage, and I wore my first real miniskirt (I loved my legs), bought in Milano the week before. He gave me roses and took me to a fine restaurant, where we ordered dinner in Italian. I thought he was exceptionally romantic, sensitive, artistic, and a whole lot of fun. He thought I was smart, outspoken, Eastern, and sophisticated.

I scared him because I was so intense and *sure* of everything. There isn't one thing that I can remember *not* having an absolute opinion about. He was not my dream man, but he walked me around Florence and talked about the Renaissance with great authority. He saw things in doorways and building façades that

I missed, and I was enchanted. He was also a terrific dancer, and there was nothing I loved more than dancing.

We spent three years courting because we were each the opposite of what we had planned for ourselves. He was as firmly Roman Catholic as I was Jewish, and my parents were opposed. His father delivered mail and there wasn't a lot of money. But more to the point, I expected that the man I married would have to win the competition—he'd be more powerful and driven than I. Clearly, Paul was not. Paul's expectations for a wife ran along the lines of his mother: she'd be a nice Catholic girl, maybe a nurse, soft-spoken, intelligent, and nurturing. My intensity, ambition and certainty attracted and repelled him. His easygoing nature, his existential confusion and fears, his depth of feeling and thought attracted and repelled me. We were married, finally, because I said we should be. We spent the first year of our marriage in Southeast Asia—he was drafted to fight the Vietnam War and I was reporting it for *Time*. I sidestepped land mines, dangled my feet off the side of helicopters, and dodged artillery fire in Cambodia, Vietnam, and Laos. It was dangerous, but I was young and very into macho.

In the first ten years of our marriage we moved annually, most often in pursuit of my journalism career, less often for his academic one. We lived in Annapolis, San Francisco, Saigon, Cleveland, Rochester, Florence again, and the District of Columbia. I reported and wrote for newspapers and magazines; he acquired a PhD in American history. We never stayed put for more than two years because, typical of the late 1960s youth generation, my operating credos were, "I never want to know where I'll be this time next year," and, "Owning property ties you down." In retrospect, I may have been fleeing the conventional values of my parents as much as I was searching for a career. The profane word in the late 1960s and early 1970s was *bourgeois*—that was what I did *not* want to be. That fear may go a way toward explaining my panic over having children. Paul always wanted them; I did not. I believed that the instant I gave birth, I would become my mother, the traditional housewife. Funny, how self-fulfilling that prophesy was.

We moved from one foreign and domestic city to another and then capitulated in a big way. We bought a thirty-five-acre farm in North Carolina, with spectacular mountain views and a two hundred-year-old rambling farmhouse in need of major renovation. We named it Tuscany Hills Farm after the province in Italy where we'd met. The idea behind the move was to escape from downtown Washington: the unbreathably torpid summer air, the urban rudeness, the high prices; the fact that our rented house had been twice burglarized, our windshield thrice smashed, and my purse snatched. The intent was to reverse the priorities of our life—instead of moving for the job, we'd make the job conform to our lifestyle. We were in search of a simpler, more human life. I had a magazine column I could write from anywhere, and Paul's research grant had just ended freeing him to move.

We delayed having children until we were both thirty-four, and we had been married eleven years. When Max was born, I had been working two years under a publisher's contract for my first book. Immediately before I gave birth, the book was killed. The blame lay with a similar book, emerging six months before mine was completed, rather than with my personal failings, but I never understood that and I was crushed. I had slaved over that book in isolation on my farm, and then I watched another author chat about *my* book on the *Today* show. I never acknowledged my extreme sense of failure. My first child was born, and I threw my energies into Max with a vengeance.

If farming was a challenge to the suburban Jewish girl, then mothering was a test for the ambitious career woman. It was another feather in my cap, another activity I could lick. And damn it, I *did*. I was a great mother to Max those first three years. "This is one child who will never make me feel guilty for the way I mother," I said more often than I now care to remember. I was proud that I balanced his needs and mine, that Paul and I—the couple—still came first.

I had proven myself professionally; these were the years to prove myself domestically—so I became the consummate rural wife. I grew, canned, and froze every vegetable and almost every piece of fruit that my family ate throughout the year. I kept chickens and collected eggs daily and had a freezer full of home-grown poultry and lamb. And I was the mother who made it all look easy, rearing the perfectly loved and loving child; Max cooperated in those years by being beautiful, friendly, and smart. Eventually I also took to entertaining in a major way. There were glorious, creative, enormous, parties for which I did all the planning, cooking, baking, and flower arranging. I took pride in my ability to put people together cleverly and make a party work. Well, by gosh, I *could* do it all.

When Max was two and a half, I started getting itchy. I began tinkering with some "urban view of the country" columns and selling them to newspapers. I was preparing to acknowledge I needed my work again, and Paul began talking about another child. His or her sole raison d'etre would be to make our happy first child even happier. But that had *not* been part of our contract; we had agreed to one child whom I would enthusiastically rear because I would never do it again. Paul was upping the ante and I was dragging my feet. But for whatever reason these things happen, I finally agreed, and damn if we didn't conceive on the first crack. So I was pregnant again.

I loved my first pregnancy, but I hated my second, and Paul's enthusiasm waned, too. The first baby had been a revelation—that we could have made this incredible little person was every bit a miracle. The second baby—dear, sweet, loving Andrew—was just a baby . . . again. There were diaper bags, car seats, bottles, feedings, and naps . . . again. Neither Paul nor I could manage the ardor for the things of babyhood we had spontaneously lavished on Max, and we were each tormented with guilt.

With Max I had been an attentive and involved mother—I was doing exactly what I wanted to be doing. I was accommodating the part of me that was lost in the frenetic career years.

"The moment I want to work, I will," I said when Max was born. I never set out to be a martyr to my child. And for two and a half years, my needs and Max's perfectly meshed.

But with Andrew I was acting out of guilt. I had been a full-time mother to Max, could I be less to Andrew? I was no longer feeling wonderfully accomplished in this all-day mothering. There was now a clear divergence of his needs and mine, and that was my dilemma.

With two small children and no work to fuel me, the gardening became drudgery. It was a lot of work and I was tired of it. Our big old dream house, with its constant renovations, became an albatross, always demanding some repair or upkeep. I came to hate dragging water to the chickens in the subzero winter and secretly hoped they would freeze to death. I was incensed when our cows broke through the board fence and trampled the roses I'd nurtured. I was furious that japanese beetles were eating our cherry trees and that we were committed to organic pest control. I came to despise the smugness of our "back to the land" friends and their idealization of the simple life. Everything made me angry: that other women handled their two children with greater ease than I, that Paul was so unambitious. In response I launched a project to convince Paul we needed a year abroad again and that the Fulbright Fellowship would be the perfect vehicle. He went through the motions, but with full awareness, he let the deadlines pass.

I pressed Paul to take action, because for the first time in my life, I was personally immobilized. After fifteen years of writing, had the devastating book defeat that coincided with Max's birth shattered my confidence? Had child rearing and life in the bucolic North Carolina mountains sapped my initiative? I expect that both are altogether possible.

When Andrew was eighteen months old, I began writing again, just two days a week—and it felt wonderful. For six solid months, I plugged away on my writing project, sent it unsolicited to the *Atlantic Monthly* and one week later started an affair with David Richard Muller.

Part I
THE BEGINNING

Monday, October 14, 1985

Late last night, I wrote this note:

David,

I think a lot about being alone with you. Does the idea intrigue you? Can it be arranged? Is it wise? Does it matter if it isn't? We've talked about ruts, gold chains, and midlife searches for adventure.

Please realize how much trust is inherent in my committing these incomplete ideas and sentences to you.

I have no idea how you will respond. I'm not sure how I would. But I do know, Dr. Muller, that the ball, as they say, is now in your court.

I.

I couldn't sleep last night wondering if I was really on the brink of acting on a fantasy I'd harbored for a year. But fantasy is one thing . . .

Tuesday, October 15

I did it. I awakened, did my Jane Fonda exercises for the first time in nine months (was this what she really had in mind?), drove to Watertown, bought a copy of *Passages,* paper-clipped my sealed letter inside the book jacket, drove to D's office with legs like rubber (so that's what *that* expression means), and forced myself to make smiling small talk with the receptionist. I told her to see that Dr. Muller got the book, and we laughed about life crises.

I felt immediately relieved. I was really driven. There was no longer any choice at all. A year ago, when the thought of making love to Dave Muller first crossed my mind, I had a choice—the idea was exciting in its own right, the idea was enough. But in this last week, when I've seen him twice, I've been obsessed with his being my lover. I slept very well tonight but awakened early and made wonderful love to Paul. Am I savoring these moments with Paul before all that is and was us is changed?

Am I thinking straighter in these days of anticipation than I ever will again? Maybe that's why it's so important, or *I think* it's so important, to write my feelings down.

So here are some of my feelings. I've never loved Paul more. I know, really know, that in this whole world there is no man better suited to be my husband.

Paul is astounded these days at how warm and loving I've been to him and I know it isn't guilt. I know that. It's a real need to affirm all that we are together, which is incredibly much. It's my way of saying that this thing I'm about to do, really *have* to do, has absolutely nothing to do with Paul and me. It has to do with me and my age, nothing more and nothing less. Dave is not more attractive to me than Paul, he is not more intelligent, he is not as well-rounded and funny and I seriously doubt that he is as good a lover. What he is, is not my husband of almost sixteen years.

Gail Sheehy wrote in *Passages:*

> Kinsey's figures showed that a wife is most likely to be un-faithful, if ever, in her late Thirties. The desire for a torrid

experience coincides with her sexual peak, which for most women is reached at about thirty-eight. And just like men, women are likely to flirt with, fantasize about, and not infrequently launch into a promiscuous phase in midlife, hoping to cure the fears, boredom, and sudden sense of bodily decline.

Falling in love or finding a new husband is not usually the point. The idea is: 'This is my last chance to have a fling before I lose my looks.'

I write all this, too, in some hope that when this falls apart, I can convince Paul that this had nothing whatsoever to do with any shortcomings in him.

The deceit is the big thing, I know, and already it has begun in big and small ways—setting up Paul for time to myself. And because Paul is so faithful and trusting, I feel twinges. But it's gone beyond that already. The die is cast. If he'll have me, I will be had.

Wednesday, October 16
All day I waited for the phone to ring, and I thought every thought from every angle. He'll call and say yes, and my heart will stop beating. He'll call and say, "I can't do that to Linda," and I'll be light-hearted and say, "It's for the best." He'll write and say no. He'll never write and never call and that will be the worst. Then I think how shocked he'll be, how he had no clue, how he gave no encouragement. Then, I think, "He's had plenty of clues, some even emanated from him a year ago."

Each time the phone rang, I could barely get the words out of my throat. And in the afternoon, when the kids were napping, the phone rang and it was his voice.

"Inette, this is Dave Muller."

"Hello, Dave Muller."

"I, uh, got the book you left, *Passages* . . ."

"You did?"

"Your timing is incredible. I really needed this. It's a time in my life when everything is going badly. I need to take a left turn. It's the most life-affirming thing that has happened to me in a long time."

"Be affirmed, David, you are an attractive man."

Then there was the swapping of available days, unavailable days, ways to get away, and it all seemed inordinately complicated. He's an obstetrician, so his days are not his own, and I've got two small children at home. This is a very, very small town. But it's clear we'll find a way, and it's so unbelievably exciting. He said he'll call again tomorrow afternoon.

Now I'm really crazy. It is not a fantasy, but it hasn't happened yet. All is anticipation now and it's driving me nuts. I just want to touch his wonderful hair, his dimple—just touch. Already I can't stand being apart. How will it be later?

Thursday, October 17

I couldn't sleep last night. I continue to be attentive to Paul. I try to fill the hours; I don't hear my son when he talks to me. I'm not a million miles away, only twenty-five.

I call the clinic and order a second diaphragm. Of course, I could ask David for one, but that seems a little tacky. I do my Jane Fondas with a vengeance for the third straight day—every pain means this body will be tighter and more attractive to David.

This is my day to write, but how can I write about anything other than the momentum that has propelled me thus far. So, what do I do now? Dave won't call until afternoon, after office hours, and I can't read or write or go out.

Questions: How will it end? Gail Sheehy says these things last about six months. They can only end badly. God, I hope Paul is spared knowing. This place is so small. I want no one to know, but what about David's partner when Dave is taking time off and then the partner tells his wife and she tells the other doctors' wives and then someone tells David's wife, Linda? You must know that I'm not stupid; I realize all the possibilities and I realize I may emerge feeling worse about myself and rejected. But none of that can influence me. This sexual energy, this need to be courted by a strange and handsome man, is not to be denied.

Tuesday, October 22

Tomorrow is the day and this has been the slowest week ever. I suffered violent swings in emotion. One day I smacked both children very hard. I've had great sex with Paul—all the while, holding my breath to keep from saying "Dave"—and this before we've even held hands. I've had lots of trouble sleeping. Those hours before I fall asleep are mine to think only of David, then I awaken early to think about him some more. It's like an intimate time alone with him, but I hate not sleeping.

This was a very social weekend, with all that is on my mind too close to the surface. I know that I'm sending signals to every male within ten feet. I feel as if I'm wearing a big red flag and the men are swarming closer than usual. I find myself making a lot of social conversation about midlife crisis and what it feels like to be thirty-nine.

There have been two phone conversations with David since I last wrote and there will be another this afternoon. The first, or our second, was awful—I felt I was going crazy not being able to touch him, wanting him to come down here to me *now*, not in a week; and I resented that he couldn't, which I interpreted as *wouldn't*. The whole physician shit, his time being so full and intractable, was really angering me—that was Thursday. But by Friday's call I had given in to his needs. Wednesdays are now his, and he reciprocated by postponing some surgery that had been scheduled for tomorrow. I did let him know how oppressive I found a physician's schedule; clearly, I am not cut out to be a docile doctor's wife.

Sunday at Ellen's baby shower, seven women sat around evaluating David Muller. My, oh my, that was strange. We gossiped about how good a doctor/person this man is who is about to become my lover. Ellen is so insightful, I wonder if she doesn't suspect.

He called just now and my heart is going like a trumpet. He told me that he just walked into a colleague's broom closet, looking for the hall door. It's reassuring that it's like that for him, too. We were going to spend tomorrow exploring the woods along the Grant County scenic drive. his old hunting and fishing spots. I loved the idea of being with him in the woods; it's what I requested. But the weather is horrible so he just told me that he booked us into the Country Inn, an hour and a half from here. The idea of a hotel room makes me very very nervous, but he couldn't have picked a more beautiful spot.

We are both so nervous and so excited. He was actually apologetic about having to work while we were on the phone today. It's awfully nice to be courted. Do all affairs involve this much anticipation? The next time I write! . . .

Thursday, October 24

Well, where to begin? First I feel really fine, just relaxed and happy and fine. If one begins a midlife affair with the express purpose of seeing oneself in the eyes of someone new, then by all measures I am successful. Dave repeats, "You are wonderful," with convincing sincerity. So who am I to doubt that I am? He loves to hear himself call me his "friend, confidante, and lover," because he is in need of all three. I am not, but I am happy to be those things to him. He is my fine lover.

I remember about nineteen years ago spending several days in Paris with Paul. But we never saw Paris, we never left bed, and we felt a bit bad about that. Paris simply couldn't compete with being stroked and kissed and held by Paul at age twenty. It was like that yesterday with David but without most of my youthful inhibitions. The hours flew past filled with caresses and tenderness beyond what I had expected. At first there were whispered names, then endearments, then confessions and confidences. It was a wholly dear and satisfying day.

The sneaking around, looking at strangers' faces for hints of familiarity, gets old fast. The trying to set meeting places where no one knows you, in a community of this size, is exasperating. But being alone in the Country Inn, a very lovely place, following a lunch with a bottle of Dom Perignon and a toast to Wednesdays, was very very satisfying.

We met at the airport north of Watertown. I got there first, waited for him to drive up, then climbed into his wife's Wagoneer. I was very nervous. David was nervous, too, and he never stopped talking. For one and a half hours we drove through the autumn foliage—David talked and I, uncharacteristically, listened. It was the first time in my life I was too scared to speak.

After lunch, I dawdled outside the Country Inn trying with no apparent success to look nonchalant as he registered us—in his own name. He had reserved a suite with a fireplace. He built a fire in the living room, and we sat on the sofa in front of the fire. I slipped off my shoes and then my earrings.

Although David and I have known each other for six years and socialized as couples for one, in many ways we're virtual strangers, neither of us knows quite what to expect. But for my part, I'm convinced that Dave is genuinely enchanted with me, surprised to be so drawn to me, and idealizing me in a wholly ego-stroking way. He says, "Inette," with a feeling and commitment I love. He finds me passionate—I'd forgotten that was a possibility. He loves to listen to my old stories of career exploits and I love to talk about them to him. Dave asked me if I believed I had a good marriage. I answered an unequivocal yes. He said, "Me too, isn't that strange? Are you too feeling your mortality? How many Wednesday afternoons are there left in life?" He later talked of being unappreciated by kids and wife, of "bringing home the bacon" to an ungrateful family, of marriage that "begins as champagne, goes flat, and perhaps with luck and time turns into fine cognac." I listened to his story but knew that it is not my own.

For me, the discoveries of and in David reinforced my decision to go ahead with this love affair. He is surprisingly sweet and sensitive, bright and searching, kind and thoughtful. I have always cast him in the role of the selfish doctor with no time for the wife or kids, no consideration of either, domineering, and even arrogant. I went into this affair thinking the worst but, nonetheless, being absolutely attracted to this man. So it is incredible to find him simply dying for the opportunity to be kind and loving and unselfish and thoughtful to me. Perhaps this interlude is a chance for him to be his best self. Perhaps he is still all those things I formerly thought, but it is very nice that the doctor self is not the David Muller who presents himself to me.

I can *feel* his needs to talk and share and hold tight to someone. He is indeed in the throes of feeling his mortality. For some reason, all of this is very compelling to me. We both enter this relationship with incredible innocence, with the belief that if we are discovered our marriages will be unharmed—"Linda just won't make dinner for a few days," he says. But it's a certainty that our affair will continue.

Paul—funny how I still feel none of this has anything to do with Paul. I know what I have in Paul, I know what we have together. Unlike David, I don't have a stagnant marriage. Paul has always been my sexual leader and still is imaginative, always pushing me beyond my own inhibitions. David is not; he is troubled by inhibitions and a strict Lutheran upbringing that he has never worked through. I sense that he will not allow me to lead him sexually, nor can he lead me. Paul is smart and creative, and Paul knows me very very well. He allows me so much room to find my own way. All of this I love—oh, I *do* love Paul and I love our marriage. Please God, let none of this be threatened by my need to see myself in a strange man's eyes. Am I actually asking God to condone adultery?

Want to hear something truly ironic? All morning I've had the strongest urge to share stories from yesterday with Paul. It's not an urge to confess in any sense, but rather a spontaneous beginning of sentences in my head, such as: "You know, David hates some of those awful hunting prints in his home, too"; or, "The Country Inn is really quite a wonderful place"; or, "We had the best champagne." I keep starting stories, intending to share them with Paul as I've always done, and then stopping myself midthought. It's funny, but so far, not sharing what I'm doing with Paul is the hardest part.

I guess I simply love having a handsome, accomplished man discovering all that is good and exciting and sexy and fascinating about me—even if I'm not fool enough to believe that what this wonderful lover sees is the real and total me.

Thursday, October 24, afternoon

Oh, Davey, the pain of your phone call just now. What have we done to you? I know the sound of cherished ideals and well-planned moves fracturing into smithereens. The sound of your distress and confusion is reminiscent of Paul's those many years ago in Florence. And I'm the catalyst for it. You can't sleep, you can't eat. You describe your feelings for me as "life itself." But there are other feelings, "in direct proportion"—remorse, guilt, fear. Can I rationalize that it's good to clear the passageways for change and growth? Dare I say that in the face of your misery and confusion? I don't know what to say to you. My writing is my therapy, my control. But you don't have that distancing perspective. Where will we go from here? And, inevitably, will my turn to suffer come? Is there no such thing as a fling? Have I been very selfish, thinking only of myself? If so, dear David, I'm truly sorry.

We won't speak again until Tuesday.

Tuesday, October 29

It's impossible to sum up a week's feelings. Today is the first time I've spoken to David since Thursday. He and Linda went to Maine on a long-planned weekend trip to search for a new practice. Then, yesterday was Paul's day off so I couldn't take a call. Starved for contact with each other, we talked and talked. It's amazing how impossible it is to keep feelings clearly in check, neatly in order. I loved it when David demanded to know over the phone exactly what I was wearing, where I was standing, where I did my writing, on what kind of machine I wrote. I love the idea of Dave obsessing about me.

An old college roommate I'd not seen for eighteen years visited here with her husband and three small sons, as planned months ago. My heart wasn't in the visit, but I went through the motions of big country breakfasts and long hikes around the farm. All weekend, surrounded by house guests, I searched for just a little space to think of Dave. I went to bed early, lay awake, and thought of his face, his hair, his dimple. David said he is feeling ennui. He said he cares little about work, life, home. He alluded to a difficult and troubled marriage. When you embark on this course, all sorts of sealed doors open. How can a marriage compete with the good face you put on for an affair? If I were as charming and devoted and thoughtful of Paul as I've been of David, my dear Paul would be shocked and thrilled.

Most of these days since last Wednesday, I have been rather devoted to Paul. Sex with him continues to be extraordinary, probably because I feel so sexy and full of myself. But yesterday I turned very bitchy, muttering, "Make it easy for me," aloud at one point.

Simply put, I need to be with David much more than I am. I can't put my whole life on hold while waiting to see him. I just pass time, ignore the children, refuse gainful activity, don't write on my writing days—but these things are happening for both of us. I don't see a resolution.

The medical practice David was checking out last weekend belonged to an OB-GYN who was run out of town on the heels of an affair and a divorce. Dave is having nightmares of no home, no wife, no job. But none of these fears can lessen our need to be together.

I know how artificial all we say and are to each other is, when held up to almost sixteen years of marriage. Paul knows me, good and bad, and really loves me—and I love him. David and I barely know each other, possibly would hate the worst in each other, but are divinely attracted and excited.

Thursday, October 31, Halloween

Today I feel a real need to write. I seem to be able to think things out on paper, and that helps. I wonder who my audience for this journal of thoughts will be. Most often I think this diary is just therapeutic, a way to establish control over events. But lately, I think that I'm writing all these thoughts and feelings only for Paul to read someday; that the habit of sharing almost everything with Paul is awfully strong, and if I'm unable to do that now, I want to be able to do it later.

Of course, I wonder about Paul's reaction to finding out about David and me. I don't know how destructive the discovery would be—to him, to us, to all the trust and faith of a lifetime together. Would it undermine his self-confidence? Would he always wonder if he were up to snuff? Would he be very angry? Would he turn deceitful and keep even more tucked inside than he already does? Would it, on the other hand, be a wonderful revelation, another shared experience, a reinforcement of us. Right now I do not want Paul and Linda to know, because that would be the end of David and me,—that road must not be closed off now.

David is, in fact, a means of self-exploration for me. He is a prism through which to see the middle-years me. I suspect that, after these five years of seeing myself reflected in my children, I need to assess myself again through the eyes of a man. Marriage just does not allow for such a reassessment after so many years of habit and accepted understandings. I'm not blind to the superficiality of the relationship with David, the holding back of commitment, the one-dimensionality of it. And still, it is altogether new and exciting and delightful.

Is it telling or is it trivial that Paul and David, Linda and I will all turn thirty-nine this year? That both couples have been married fifteen years—all born in 1946 and all married in 1970?

It's funny how much I find myself thinking about those earlier years with Paul and before him: the last time I tormented myself with thoughts of men and boys and how they relate to me; the last time I felt hours of unbearable sexual tension and frustration;

the last time I posed for a man, set up an image of myself I would want him to have and hold, at the expense of his own findings and observations. I dress a certain way to elicit a certain response from a certain man, I move a certain way, tell certain stories to establish my cleverness—it's all so self-concerned, so endlessly egocentric.

Stroking is what this is all about, my endless midlife need to be stroked. Dave, stroke my face, my arm, my thirty-nine-year-old ego. Tell me I am desirable and lusty and incredibly attractive and bright. Tell me there is no one like me. Say my name over and over, husky and full or yearning. Just writing this makes my breath short.

I try to hold myself open to the possibility that this affair could end tomorrow. But I don't want it to. And I fear that, when it does, I won't be ready. In my heart of hearts, I know it's a course that will be run, serving a purpose for a time and then no more. And of course, that must be the case for Paul and me to continue to be married and family until we die.

Sometimes I ask myself what it is about me that needs these two men—not one and not the other, but both. David alone would be completely unsatisfactory; Paul alone at this point in my life leaves me without the excitement and self-affirmation that I absolutely crave. I do know that I won't always crave these things. I *have* not for all these many years, and I feel fairly certain that a time will again come when I don't need that second man. But now, I'm happier, fuller, and more alive for there being a David Muller on Wednesdays.

David came to my home yesterday for a couple of midday hours. I hated for him to leave. He left me climbing the walls, full of sexual energies unexpended. I thought I'd go mad the rest of the day, scurrying around setting up babysitters for next Wednesday. My focus is Wednesday to Wednesday; it's a weird way to spend my weeks. Everything in between is an obstacle to the next meeting. So children, trick-or-treating, soccer games, visits with friends, book discussion club meetings, dinners prepared and eaten become events to get past; roadblocks to kissing David Muller.

Years ago, someone said to me that gynecologists are women haters. I wonder if this is true of David. He talks about doctors' wives with such scorn, and in response to one of my questions, he answered, "Who knows, they're women." I expressed some outrage, gave the feminist lecture on these doctors' wives who are caught in the web of being kept by supporting men, whose only measure of worth is their husband's net income. He is unsympathetic. He sees them as lesser creatures. So, does he hate women and am I temporarily exempt because of my more masculine drive, ambition, and independence? If I appear vulnerable, will he hate me, too? If I am too pushy, will I threaten him? All these issues are resolved with Paul, thank God, and I'm not crazy about figuring them out again with David. But that's part of this package, I understand.

Paul loves women, almost all women, more than he loves men. I'm absolutely certain this is because he was crazy about his mother. Years ago, my friend Susan said that the best husbands are men who loved their mothers—the mamas' boys so to speak. As time passes, that becomes my gospel; it's an absolute. Paul loved his mother and he loves me and he genuinely appreciates women and their subtleties. David and his mother are still a question. He's talked about his father, but the only mention of his mother came when I put my finger in his dimple and asked him if people were always putting their fingers in his dimple, and he said, "My mother used to do that." David thinks of himself as a man's man, I believe: hunting, fishing, shooting big game, competing with other male doctors. In some way, that's very attractive to me, for the difference of it, the alienness. In other ways, it's distancing, a way that men separate themselves from their women.

In some obvious ways, David and I are similar where Paul and I are not. We are both competitive, self-centered, unsacrificing, arrogant, and controlled. Last night, Paul and I were talking about the mythology surrounding Jewish women and their sexuality. There is, he said like the academic he is, "the one strand of thinking that holds Jewish women to be warm and highly sexual; there is the other image of the Jewish princess, shallow and self-absorbed—and who wants to make love to that?" I feel closer to the latter with David and I'd rather not have that image. I do want to work at some level of exposure and vulnerability in this relationship, but I just don't know. I suspect that if David can see his way clear to reach out, to open up, to share, then I will respond. But if he does not—I don't know . . .

I sent this letter, without a return address, to David's office today.

Halloween, 1985
My dear dear David,
The time has come to stop writing only about you and to begin writing to you. I suspect this is something I have wanted to do for some time, restrained only by the logistics of getting this letter to you. Perhaps you can direct me in a method.

After we spoke, your reference to the *Atlantic Monthly* poem had completely slipped my mind. Only now, several hours later did I remember. What a lovely poem. Yes, it is *us*. I do like saying *us*. Why is it that it never occurred to me that you read poetry? Why is it that I persist in thinking of you as the doctor, the hunter, the male. You have no idea, I think, of the strength of my defenses, of my need to feel control. Understanding this, you begin to understand why it's important to me to define you in a certain way that doesn't threaten my tranquillity and, more to the point, my marriage.

Yet, every now and again, you do break through and I realize what a disservice I do you. Knowing that you read that lovely poem, thought of "us," and sent it on to me is one of those moments.

If you read what I've been writing about you, about Paul and about me, you would, at the least, be perplexed. I'm very uncertain where you and I are headed, but I am certain that I choose to be powerless in preventing wherever it is we are going. Under no circumstances do I want to climb off this particular train. And yet, all the while, in my writing I'm struggling to maintain categories and equilibrium: as in, Paul is *this* and David is *that.*

When you are your most vulnerable, I'm most unable to maintain my categories and distinctions. When you are your most confused, I'm most touched. When you're most preoccupied with me, I'm most obsessed with you.

There's so very much we don't know about each other. And I thought that's the way I wanted it to be—a measure of distance and a measure of control. But that is not the way I feel right now. I feel a bit like crying and I know it would be very nice to cry in your arms.

Inette

Friday, November 1

Maybe I'm just very tired, dragging around all day trying to entertain two small children. Maybe I'm just tired of rearing small children and weary of the demands they make. Maybe I'm in a premenstrual funk. Maybe. But the fact is that, as the children nap in the car, I race to this typewriter to say that I just seem to care much less about all the things I've always cared a great deal about: my children, my community, my marriage. Perhaps this is the dynamic of an affair. It takes center stage, it emotionally dwarfs all competing pulls. Nothing can compete with the intense drama of an adulterous affair.

That is where I am. I simply want to get into the car with David and drive away—away from children, home, hearth, and love-of-my-life Paul. And for what? I want to leave just to leave— for the space to myself, for the uninterrupted time with David, for the chance to find what Dave and I offer each other.

I will take greater risks and increase the chance of discovery to ensure uninterrupted time with David Muller, and I simply don't know why.

In some ways I believe I am very, very lucky to have found a

Dave Muller, with all his qualities and interests, at a time in my life when I'm so in need. In this backwater, I have found someone who offers me so much. Maybe David Muller is the only way I'll survive, get through this time of life that's demanding and unrewarding (small children, small town, no niche of my own). Maybe that's all there is to it—the right man to supplement my life at the right time. Or maybe he's the monkey wrench that will shatter everything I've neatly arranged in my life. Maybe all that was and is will be no more. Maybe I'm on the brink of a major midlife emotional crisis. Shit, I hate the turmoil.

Saturday, November 2

It has never been worse. I'm nonfunctional. I can't do a thing. I'm completely lethargic; everything and everyone gets on my nerves. All I've done this entire day is lie on the sofa and try to read (I've begun and abandoned a half-dozen books). I think only about David—and all I think about David is how much I need to talk to him and how angry I am at myself for not figuring out a way to have him call me this weekend, when he asked. Now Paul has taken both children out for dinner, leaving me alone at least, and all I can think about is "How can I call David? At home? At the hospital? At the office? How, how, how?"

This business of secrecy puts severe restraints on the times and places I can see David—or even hear his voice. So far it works like this: We meet on Wednesdays after surgery, around ten A.M., at the county airport and drive off to distant places. He says, "I'll call you Thursday at noon." We talk for fifteen minutes, at most. Because Paul is home Saturday afternoon, Sunday, and Monday, I can't receive David's calls then. He calls again on Tuesday at noon and we speak for another intense fifteen minutes. Thursday to Tuesday, we both suffer. Now we've added the layer of the written word. David writes me at home on plain tan stationery, and I am absolutely certain to pick up the mail before Paul does. I write David at his office or put the letter into his parked Jeep at his office parking lot. (David uses a four-wheel drive Jeep for work, his wife drives a Wagoneer, and he keeps a

Jaguar sedan in his garage for special trips.) We live twenty-five miles apart, he's in a town of three thousand, I'm in a town of five hundred. I normally go to his larger town to shop, but he has no legitimate reason to be seen in my little farm town.

I *cannot* wait until Tuesday to hear his voice. I am going completely crazy. Paul looks at my behavior and tells me I should take up drinking. "If a doctor looked at your symptoms," Paul says, "he'd put you on Valium." It's true. I *cannot* wait until Wednesday—how many hours, how many days until then? How many activities have to be dispensed with, how many words spoken to how many people? How many nights to sleep through? I can't bear this. Yikes, I want to scream it out—Dave, Dave, Dave!

I feel worthless. At least David is delivering babies, functioning. I feel as if I'm vegetating. Nothing at all can help me get through these interminable days between now and Wednesday. David, hear my scream and call—*please, please call.*

Thursday, November 7

Paul is away on business, so I had the luxury of David all day yesterday and the peace and freedom to indulge myself in thoughts of David all night. I'm free of the restraints of Paul's presence. I've never before been happy that Paul's away.

I feel wonderful. What I feel, what I haven't allowed myself to say aloud, what I'm only now murmuring in my brain is, "I feel like a girl falling in love." I'm falling in love, and it's the most satisfying, filling, enhancing, tingling feeling in the world. Maybe the problem with these middle years is just that we've forgotten what it is to fall in love. And other than the act of giving birth, or going to war, nothing else is as total, as electrifying. Maybe there are consequences of these feelings, and maybe there should be accompanying pangs and constrictions, but at this moment there are none. Paul is in Raleigh, the children are at school and sitter, Dave will call at noon, and I feel star touched and totally happy. I'm so light, I'm so full, I'm so free of ambivalence.

All day yesterday while we made love, when David so completely appreciated me and my body, I felt a recurring urge to say, "I love you," but I held back. I thought, "No, this isn't love, it's passion speaking." I thought, "No, it would be inappropriate to say these things, it would be another burden on David."

All night I lay in bed and reveled in thoughts of David, delighted in the subtleties that are David Muller. It is very nice to be discovering this man. It is also very, very nice to watch him discovering me. Should I write and tell Dave these feelings? Is it possible that I would not? Will the word *love* send up a red flag and put fear in David's heart? Are we beyond such flags and fears at thirty-nine? Suddenly I love being thirty-nine and I feel that it took all these years just to arrive at this point.

Tuesday, November 12
I just ran the half-mile up to the mailbox in hope of a letter from Dave. Instead there was a *New York Times* rejection, so I am twice bummed.

Sunday was a very peculiar day. Paul and I, David and Linda—our first social excursion as couples since the affair. At one point, at a harp concert, I sat wedged between Paul's and David's shoulders and knees. Obviously, I have no idea what the concert was about. I sat there thinking, "Dave . . . oh, Dave," and feeling the paranoid certainty that Linda must be reading my mind and Paul my feelings. But no one was.

All afternoon and evening at the Mullers' home, I was with David but not *with* David. I was looking at Paul critically through David's eyes. I watched Paul hole up, intimidated by the man who Paul said, "delivers babies, builds furniture, hunts, fishes, rides horses." Paul does none of these things, and I felt bad that he couldn't relax and show his best self. Oh, the competition for macho. David looked kind of smug at the end of the evening, I thought.

I guess—no, I know—it's better to see David than not to. But it's so very hard to see him, be with him, and have this enormous distance. The coupling of four seems to work well, and though neither is a person that Paul naturally warms to, he will try. Linda is too repressed for Paul's taste and David appears too slick. Linda seems to feel warmth for me. David tries to be gracious and courteous to Paul, but is it possible to genuinely like and respect the man whose wife you're sleeping with?

Thursday, November 14

Yesterday was the most wonderful day of all. We were alone in a tiny log cabin in the woods and mountains two hours north. There was a fire in the fireplace warming the chilly cabin, steaks David cooked for dinner, and bunk beds for making love. The love making was better than ever—David and I are warming to this thing. We exchanged stories of our families, our youth, and things that were: old politics, old schools, old jobs. We talked a lot, we kissed even more. He is a slow and attentive lover. He has his inhibitions, but he also has all the time in the world— there's no rush to where we're going.

In response to my Halloween letter, David confessed yesterday, "I am hopelessly and inextricably in love." Somehow, the saying that we're in love makes things very different. On the long ride home in the dark, after what was the most perfect day for each of us, I couldn't let go of the questions: "Where is it we are heading? What will happen if we are discovered?" He finally was pushed to answer, "I believe our marriages will survive but we will not." So it's clear. We have everything invested in discretion. Funny, I know I wouldn't leave Paul, but I still wanted to hear David say that he would leave Linda. Yet I know he could not—in fact, should not.

He says he is "spoiled" by his marriage. He says, "You would never put up with my job, my hours." We agree that we're very alike in many, many ways.

David has booked us flights to Boston for some medical meeting. I've been pushing for this—extended time together—and yet I can't believe that we're going to do it. I told Paul that I'm visiting my friend Carol in Washington for a few days; David has gone to considerable lengths to discourage Linda from accompanying him to the meeting. It's all rather unreal: So many lies, such uncharacteristic deceit for David and me, and yet it seems so inevitable. Paul, will you ever ever understand how inevitable this all is? This trip will happen in three weeks. The idea of sitting next to each other on a plane, of walking big-city streets hand-in-hand without fear of discovery, of sleeping curled together throughout the night is unbelievable and exhilarating.

David has lost a whole lot of weight since October 23. Yesterday he told me his belt is four holes in. And remembering I had told him that Paul had wasted away after we met in Florence those twenty years ago, David asked, "Do you always have this effect on men?"

David has never complimented a single physical quality of mine. Maybe he doesn't give compliments easily. He writes that I am sensitive and sensual and passionate. But I wish he would love the way some part of me looks and tell me. I also wish that he would tell me in explicit detail what it is he loves about me. I'll probably ask at some point.

Friday, November 15

I guess things between David and me have turned a corner. I find my loyalties subtly shifting from Paul to Dave. Where earlier I refused to discuss Paul with David because it felt like a betrayal, now I will. Where before my time with Paul was valued and valuable, now it's expendable—a tradeoff I willingly make for time to see David, to think of David. I gave David my unpublished manuscript to read: in itself an act of trust and, because of Paul's heavy editing help, still another betrayal. He called today to tell me how very much he enjoyed the story—"It was so *you*, so direct and honest." He told me that reading the manuscript was like being with me. And now I find myself thinking, "Paul never liked the way I write, never really appreciated my writing." But others have, and David does. Paul values what I accomplish, but not what I write. This is my first betrayal in thought—a significant comparison, with David coming out ahead.

And now, further betrayal—I want to tell David my thought.

Yes, we've turned a corner. I have almost sixteen years invested in this marriage, this love of Paul, this family we've created, plus another three and a half with Paul before marriage—almost twenty years. Look what a month of infidelity does. I think that embarking on an affair is so very dangerous. I don't think I understood the possibilities before. Now that I know them, how is it that I can say, "I'd do it again, I could not do otherwise."?

I love loving David. I love his loving me. I love being just us two people—no children, no mortgages, no dirty house—together. The more I know of him, the more I like him. I love to look at his face, his wonderful glowing face.

Saturday, November 16
I sent this letter to David's office today.

My dear David,
How can loving someone and being loved by them ever do harm? I think it cannot. I hope not. Confusion, even craziness perhaps, are tools of needed change. And change, slow evolution over twenty years or incredibly eye-opening jolts like this one, is really what life is all about. Better to cry a little, hurt a little, and love a lot than never to feel a thing. Even if all of this sounds trite, I do wholeheartedly believe it. My reading is, you're a man who's needed to be totally, absolutely, and yes, passionately loved for a long time. All of this clear-thinking, certain prose is not to be confused with clear thinking in *me*.

I can know all of this inside of me, but what I feel, rest assured, is what you say you feel: "Elated, frightened, dizzy, confused, and yet wondrously happy, completely enraptured with you." Yet more and more I'm really willing to throw my fate to the wind; to let what'll be, be; not to hold back; not to dwell on the possible harm or destruction.

Right now I tend to accept that this is what life has written up for me. For now, I'll dwell on my good fortune and on how simply terrific it feels to be full of love for you—to be loved by you. The rest will have to sort itself out because there is nothing I can do to clarify things. And there is nothing I'm willing to do to make things as they were before we loved.

Of one thing I am absolutely certain—I will always think of you with enormous yearning and love, regardless of where I am and what my circumstances.

                                                    Inette

Thursday, November 21

Paul is flying to Kansas City where he'll be until late Sunday. He left yesterday morning saying he'd call Friday night, "Although you'll probably be out with a handsome man."

Which brings me to the point of my handsome man. David and I had our longest and most glorious day together yesterday. It was a return trip to the Country Inn (thanks to the romantic in Dave). We met as usual at the county airport. This time David drove his Jaguar and it's a genuinely fine car, only partially wasted on someone without highly developed car sensibilities. But it does smell wonderfully like leather and it can glide along effortlessly at high speeds.

All of this is prelude to the fact that David and I are totally, irrevocably in love. Every day together is a quantum leap better than the day before. Last week—or maybe before—I turned a corner when I decided to put my guilt aside, to set my love and loyalty to Paul on a shelf, to ignore my kids' needs, and simply *go for it* in this relationship. Maybe there was never a choice, maybe I could never have held back as I assumed I would in this affair. Maybe it's my nature to be perfectly selfish and deny myself nothing, or maybe it's in the nature of an affair that these choices to give or to hold back are not choices at all.

Nevertheless, yesterday there was such candor, such sharing, such an absence of game playing, such a genuine appreciation of one another. It's easy to talk to Dave about virtually anything. In everything I share, I see an opening and reaching out from him. I feel so adored, so treasured, so loved. "I wouldn't change a single thing about you," he said at one point. It's so funny—

my being Jewish and urban are very much how David sees me.
"You just aren't a country girl," he laughed. "But I try so hard,"
I answered. He really does love everything he sees in me and I
guess I also love everything I see in him. This, despite the fact
that he seems a detached father, a selfish husband. But these
things are hard to assign guilt to. Linda and David's marriage is
very traditional: the kids are hers, the responsibility for keeping
the dead flies swept up is hers, the making of money is his. "I
don't know why we stay married," Linda told him years ago when
he admired an attractive woman. "All I ever wanted was a knight
in shining armor and all you ever wanted was a sexpot."

After their first child was born, David escaped on weekends
by skiing, worked longer hours, abdicated his responsibility for
the kids. With his son, David allows no leeway—he's his own
domineering father. He is very into measuring success by money,
the doctor thing. He wants me to know that money is very, very
important. These values all relate to his father and their relationship. His mother was the upholder of Lutheran morality and
her big fear was not so much for his success—which she assumed—but that his testosterone would win out and he'd marry
an "inappropriate girl." Linda was not inappropriate; I suspect
that I would be very inappropriate. David's single strong emotional attachment is for his daughter. He said, "I often wonder
how Debra would feel about you." I said, "She'd hate me for
harming her parents' marriage." He said, "I don't know, I think
she would like this woman who makes her father so happy." But
I know better.

What is so grand about falling in love at thirty-nine is that
there's such an absence of baloney or bullshit. We keep laying
our ugliest selves on the table for the other to know. It seems
we're totally unafraid of being rejected if we reveal our undersides.
Of course, if we are rejected, we still have our marriages—there
isn't a dark, cold void.

David studied piano seriously throughout his childhood and
college years. He thought he was very, very good until at fourteen
he went to a competition in Chicago and was crushed. His

mother saw music as his entree into the better classes. David is
very bright and well rounded. I haven't found an area he doesn't
know about: Hemingway, Bergman, Milton Friedman. I, at least,
am far better traveled. I do have fine taste in men.

And sex—this is an area where I thought David might not
knock my socks off. Well, cancel that thought. Wow! Yesterday,
making love over and over, tirelessly, attentively—it takes my
breath away. I could kiss David forever. In this passion to touch,
to never stop running my fingers through his great hair, to hold
his hand, to always have a piece of him—I recognize the early
days with Paul. I do know how unfair it is to hold an almost
sixteen-year marriage up to this sort of comparison.

On the drive home David said, "Paul is a fine person. If only
he were a shit this would be easier." I have listed Paul's good
qualities to David in some detail: Paul is funny, smart, a great
husband, and a terrific father.

So, why am I in love with this new man? I mean, *seriously* in
love. Dave called first thing this morning to check if I'd gotten
home safely last night and to tell me, "I am completely and
totally in love with you." I stood there in the kitchen, with the
children eating their breakfast, and whispered love messages into
the phone.

I have decided to give this relationship a fair and honest
opportunity to develop as it will. Can it get still better? Will it
peak and taper off if it's uninterrupted by discovery? I asked David
hypothetically what would happen if our plane to Boston crashed
and everyone found out what we've been up to. "In that case,"
he said, "it wouldn't matter. We would become a Wagnerian
opera." Would discovery make us defend the relationship? Will
we reach a point when it is essential to reveal the affair to seize
more time together? Time together seems to be the crucial issue.
Simply put, I want to be with Dave every minute of every day.
Our need to be together may force this issue in ways we may not
wish.

I don't understand how David can stay in the marriage he

describes: they never fight, can't talk, rarely make love. I can't see it, whether or not he and I continue. Paul and I are a whole different issue—he remains the man who is my best possible husband. But lately I've been picking enormous fights with Paul. He thinks the fights are related to his increased business travel. In fact, I fight so we won't have to make love before I see Dave, and because I feel guilty. But I explain my erratic behavior this way: "I'm going through this terrible anxiety-producing midlife crisis and all I can think about is me." It's the nature of this search for midlife definition, I tell Paul, that makes me resent having to do so much for him or for the kids. All of this is, of course, absolutely true—but incomplete. With this explanation, we settled our bad feelings before he left and we stayed up late enough to avoid making love.

Is there some way that I can take a leave of absence from my life and spend an extended period—say, a year—with Dave, just checking out what it is we have, free of the pressures of time and discretion? David fantasizes this taking place in an inner-city apartment in a funky Pakistani or orthodox Jewish neighborhood in Chicago with a yacht docked on the lake. Or he fantasizes us in Marrakech. I fantasize us with uninterrupted time together in the woods, with David teaching me to hunt and fish. I fantasize Dave teaching me about his music. In short, he imagines me in urban or exotic places, I guess because I am urban and exotic to him. I place us in male and rural domains because his interests are so male.

I'm not as uncaring and unfeeling as I sound. I am simply physically, emotionally, and intellectually in love—tell me how I can let such a stroke of good fortune pass. I now understand why there's a prohibition on love affairs. The "zipless fuck" was what I thought I wanted, but David Muller, this wonderful loving and loved man, is what I got. *Selfish* doesn't even begin to describe Dave and me in our respective families. There are many things I kind of know intellectually, but it seems remarkably easy to ignore and repress them.

Sunday, November 24

I have just now received a letter from David that I believe has changed my life.

My Dearest Inette,

I finished the delivery that I was waiting on when I called you; I'm still thinking of you and so I write. Inette, I feel so wonderful about you, about us, and my joy over you seems only capable of increasing. The hints of remorse that I wrote to you about at the beginning have disappeared. I am reminded of the Shakespearean sonnet that I remember (poorly) from high school. "Do not to the marriage of true minds admit impediments." The only "impediment" that I now hold sacred is that I feel duty-bound to protect the trust and honor that have been shown to me. Clearly, I have a great and increasing appreciation for the level of trust you have placed in me, your vulnerability in this, and your degree of risk-taking. And for all this I feel doubly honored, doubly lucky, and love you all the more.

I was fascinated by the "primordial history" of our relationship that you related to me this evening. There is no doubt that I had an intense interest in you from the first moment we met. I feel even now that this interest was deep and near subconscious, and yet Linda has perceived otherwise. I cannot believe my great obtuseness at your early messages. But it was not the message or even my Midwestern prudishness that prevented my response; rather, it was my lack of faith, my inability to believe that anyone of your intelligence, your strength of character would really have been interested in me. When I received your first letter, it was like an explosion within me—and yet I remained skeptical. I remained doubting until we were alone together in that room in the Country Inn. I then knew immediately and with sudden impact that we shared a feeling that was deep, profound, and genuine. It was with great fear and trembling that I touched you at that moment, Inette, a moment full of realization that nothing would ever be the same for me.

From that moment I would never think, feel, or see anything

the same as before: not about you, myself, or the entire world. You are wonderful, Inette. I am absolutely certain that no one else on earth would have made me feel this way. Whatever I have wanted or needed and could not gain from my work, my family, or my community, I have gained from you. For whatever else may happen, I love you eternally for this.

Forever, your friend, confidante and lover,
Dave

Yesterday Dave came over to my white clapboard farmhouse early in the morning. I sent the boys out to a babysitter's house. We had from nine A.M. to five P.M. completely to ourselves here. It was bright and sunny, perfectly autumnal, and we had a fire in the library and a lovely lunch in the dining room (omelets, croissants, wine, and brownies). But almost every other moment of the day was spent in my large, canopied bed on my white eyelet sheets. David had no inhibitions about being in my marital bed and I repressed mine. It was a sexual day unlike any other in my life—so much, so continuously, and so increasingly wonderful. What a lover. What a surprise. It's as though we grow together sexually as we grow together in all other ways.

David loves that I touch his face. I fell asleep briefly still touching his face. "Like the first stages of anesthetic, your fingers kept moving," my doctor-lover said. I love when he touches my curls.

I love Paul's not being here. It frees me to be with David, even when David is not here. I went to bed at seven P.M. after I put the kids down—to be in the bed where Dave had been, where we had been, to smell the pillowcases, to remember.

And now the letter I received from him today explicitly describing his feelings takes me yet another step in my commitment to David. I lie here while the children nap and imagine—for the first time, imagine—life without Paul, life outside this family. And I cry a little that the thought—the heretical thought—has crossed my mind. And I want now to ask Dave, "Could you leave Linda?" And I think, "Do I leave clues for Paul so the shock won't be so great or do I hang on until there's absolute certainty and then explain?" Can there ever be absolute certainty? Will I live to regret this?

I have heard a woman in a second marriage say, "You marry this person and you're grateful for all the new and different things he is, but you take for granted that all the qualities of your first husband will be there. And when they are not, you are shocked and disappointed."

Oh, David—is it possible that I'm actually thinking and writing this? Will having thought and then written this change things even more? Will you awaken one day and see that I'm not all the good things you think I am—that I'm phony, pompous, silly, pretentious, and selfish? Will David awaken one day and not love me, leave me alone and severed from Paul? Will Paul come home tonight and restake his claim on me?

Would Dave and I be so wonderful together, if we were totally free to be together? Surely the secrecy and the infrequence enhance the romance and sharpen the feelings. Would it be better if we were free to walk down the street holding hands? Would marriage kill all that's exciting and caring and tender in us? Should we just seize what we can have of each other now and for as long as we can, and let the rest go?

Everything feels very different after Dave's letter. Every letter, every phone call, every day and hour together moves us further along. Is it a river on an unalterable course? Are we inevitable? Is David Muller everything I need to complete the rest of my life? God, I could cry. I *am* crying at these very intense feelings. David, I *love* you.

I will send this letter to David's office.

Dear Dave,

For years I have divided the world into men who will tell you what you want to hear to gain some advantage, and those like Paul who tell you very little with words but are 100 percent sincere. You are a totally other thing for me—completely sincere *and* willing to let me know what you feel. You are a revelation.

Thank you, thank you for your letter, for your love, for your life.

With the deepest of love,
Inette

Tuesday, November 26

I am having my first serious pangs of paranoia and I don't like the feeling at all. Yesterday I took my son Max to the ophthalmologist at David's medical clinic to get a speck of rust out of his eye. Was it my imagination that my friend and pediatrician Daniel Lucas was less than friendly? Was it my imagination that one of the nurses appeared to stare through the window at me in a most intent and analytical way? I felt very conspicious.

Several weeks ago a frightening thing happened. The owner of an inn where David had booked us reservations in his own name, using his own American Express card, called his office and reported to his secretary, "The hotel room Dr. Muller booked in Petersburg for Wednesday is forced to cancel because of flooding and I'll try to find him another room nearby." David's secretary sashayed down the hall to the examining rooms, with an enormous grin on her face, and announced in full voice in front of David's partner and two nurses: "Dr. Muller, your hotel room for tomorrow in Petersburg is canceling because of flooding." David, who undoubtedly blanched, said, "I don't know what you're talking about." Too little, too late. Within minutes, a hunting buddy physician was giving David the elbow and needling, "You sure ain't shooting birds tomorrow."

Of course, since that incriminating phone call, these people have been talking among themselves about David's affair. He walks into the nurses' lounge now and the buzz of chatter turns to dead, dead silence. But I have felt apart from that. There's no way that I could be implicated. How could they put us together? Yet perhaps I am naïve: there are letters with my town's postmark, phone calls from his office to me, notes I place on the seat of his car, casual encounters in the clinic hallways on my way to see other doctors. Of course, I'm still uncertain, and only if Dave were confronted would I be convinced that I'm suspect, but it's truly a sickening feeling—the prospect of being the butt of gossip and condemnation.

Paul is back from Kansas City. I have definitely pulled back. My loyalties are shifting. He came home and insisted on making love late that night. I feigned sleep, but it was unavoidable and a sham. We've shared very little about the trip or my days without him; I'm using the children to avoid communication.

Next week is Boston, but will we ever get to that? So much happens in a week.

Wednesday, November 27
I sent this letter to David tonight.

My dear David,
It is the day we met at noon for lunch. I sit here surrounded by your literary points of reference: *For Whom the Bell Tolls*, *Beowulf*, T. S. Eliot's "Portrait of a Lady." I raided the library after I left you.

There's been a lot of stress this evening. Max had an ear infection and spent all day screaming in pain at day care. They tried to reach me and couldn't. Paul was at work too far away, so they called our lawyer friend Louis. He kept the screaming, feverish Max on his office couch all afternoon. I swooped in at 4:30 P.M., then dashed to the doc and then to the pharmacy— filled with guilt. I'm oppressed that my child was in pain while I drew my own sustenance from you and then from your books. But concurrently, I feel deep resentment that it's *me* who feels guilty for not being with *our* sick child—and I turn that on Paul.

But let me put that to rest. I sit here in my bathrobe, snuggled over in one corner of the living room sofa, and read what you read. I'm rereading the La Gloria scene in *For Whom the Bell Tolls* . . .

"Then they were together so that as the hand of the watch moved, unseen now, they knew nothing could ever happen to the one that did not happen to the other, that no other thing could happen more than this; that this was all and always; this was what had been, and now and whatever was to come," said Hemingway and David Muller.

I'm touched that in this most beautiful of love scenes, you see us. I'm overwhelmed by the depth of your mind and your heart— continually I'm surprised to find this mixture of sensitivity, intellect, charm, and humanity in you.

You speak of being "awestruck" by me, and I insist we mustn't do that to one another—yet I, too, am full of awe for the man you are.

I feel as though all that is you is substantial and solid and rooted—full of connections and understanding, full of intelligence, but clearly not a slave to the intellect. And then there's me. Self-deprecation isn't my strong suit, so bear with me—I'm neither a setter of trends nor a fuser of past connections. It's this middling journalist ground I inhabit—I'm not exactly a dilettante, but neither am I as great a thinker as I would very much like to be.

Dave, I love just about everything I know of you and I'm very excited by the prospect of knowing more, of knowing it all. I'm so proud to be in love with you, that you're in love with me. Isn't *proud* a funny word to choose? And your face—today at lunch, I simply couldn't take my eyes from your face. Do you know that I've never before in my life loved the looks of a man or boy who I loved? Of course, in Paul's case, as years passed, I grew to love certain physical qualities. But you—is there such a thing as objective handsomeness and are you undeniably that? The idea makes me nervous—the whole world agreeing that you are handsome. I'd rather believe that there is a subjective attitude, that in *my* eyes alone you are very, very beautiful.

Physical beauty is a funny thing. I always knew that I looked all right. My mother liked to call me *attractive* (a far cry from *beautiful*). But girls were so conditioned to primp and to compete over the attentions of men, and our faces and bodies were the medium of exchange for attention. Early on I knew that personality and intellect were what I'd offer in exchange—that I had to redefine the marketplace. And I guess I did. But I would love to be beautiful for you and to you.

Ah David, we've come so far, so fast, together. There's very little I can't or won't say to you. I do want to be the best of me for you. But I also want to be the whole of me for you—not chosen little pieces.

Dave, I too am perplexed, as you say you are by me, that you love me as you do—that you've given yourself over to me so freely. I'm amazed and ecstatic.

We're indeed very lucky.

I love you very much, dear David,
Inette

Part II
TURNING

Thursday, December 5

David's wife Linda saw him off at the Watertown airport on his private flight to Asheville, connecting with a commercial jet to the Boston medical conference. This was the first time Linda hadn't accompanied David to a meeting. Paul waved me off for my drive to visit Carol in Washington. In fact, I drove the two hours to the Asheville airport where David met me. Two plane tickets were booked at David's office for Dr. and Mrs. David Muller—the excuse at the office was that Linda backed out at the last moment. So I flew as Linda. We held hands and climbed aboard our flight to Boston. I bought brand-new luggage, underwear, perfume and a nightgown for the trip.

I write the journal today on hotel stationery in the room David and I will share for three nights and four days in Boston. We flew here from Asheville yesterday morning—the plane did not crash, so we're not yet a Wagnerian opera. Yesterday was the finest day of my life.

David is a superfine lover: attentive, gentle, thoughtful, indulgent, and with the most incredible energy I've ever experienced—a man of consummate energy. He awakens totally bright eyed, he requires very little sleep, he falls asleep quickly and economically—the perfect obstetrician. So we've spent our first night together, in my new-for-the-occasion pink satin nightshirt (and pearls), and it was glorious.

Dinner last night in the hotel dining room (we chose not to go far) was slow, French and delicious—filled with most serious talk of us and compatibility and futures. What future? How? David needed to know if a woman of my nature (demanding of her man's time) could make concessions to a man with his job (also demanding of his time). I answered: "If you remain this eager to see me and love me when you come home, if you are head-over-heels in love when you walk through the door—then I can learn to live with the separations." With that out of the way, Dave plunged into the fray, talked futures.

But I write now at five P.M., not from the glory that is us, but from a bad case of about-to-get-my-period blues. And for the first time they're directed at David; I'm feeling my first bad feelings about David. The reason: David purportedly came here for a medical meeting on lasers, but he always professed extreme ambivalence about actually attending the meetings; I always retorted that it'd be a test of my unselfishness if I allowed him to go. Well, he went. He's been gone since 7:15 A.M. and tomorrow is another all-day meeting. Saturday afternoon we go home.

I can't get it out of my mind—our time, our precious time together, wasted apart. These days that are free of the fear of recognition, free of curfews—and *he* chooses to impose separation and curfews. In my heart of hearts, I wanted him to give me no choice, to tell me there's no way on God's earth that he could piddle away our time together on lasers.

Last night when we went to bed, I hated that there would be a wake-up call, a quick few minutes, and then he would be gone. This morning, I was philosophical: I enjoyed the privacy of the shower, the time to read the paper, and the idea of exploring Boston—or so I told myself. In fact, I wanted to be exploring and discovering with the man I love. But I plugged on until I was exhausted. Then I walked over to the art museum for a noon lunch with David. He was a half-hour late and I thought, "Damn it, I'm *still* waiting for him." I came close, but not very, to disappearing and hopping a plane back to North Carolina.

Saturday, December 7

David walked into the hotel room Thursday and found me writing passionately and with great anger into this journal. I spilled my fury, told him what I'd written, and he was immediately and completely remorseful—adamant that he would not complete the conference. He did not.

Boston with David was extraordinary: we walked where we wished, held hands, and kissed without fear of being observed. We were complete tourists: sightseeing, window-shopping, and walking from one end of the city to the other. We spent one evening at the orchestra and I loved watching David savor the music—I loved his music myself. Last night's dinner was story-book perfect in an old section of town, at a tiny French bistro dripping atmosphere and crawling with lovers.

A funny story did come out of that laser conference. David raced across town Thursday to meet me for lunch and then killed himself to get back to the meeting on time. He arrived back a bit late and explained to a colleague that he'd met his wife for lunch at the museum. The colleague studied old Dave's face and queried, "Are you sure this was your wife?"

The four days passed and it became increasingly clear to each of us that Wednesday afternoons would never again be enough. How could a few hidden hours a week be sufficient after awakening next to each other, eating breakfast together (To my shock, he ordered white bread with his eggs and then said defensively, "There's enough exotic in my life right now."), and moving about freely and publicly?

David was unequivocal. He wanted an end to the deceit. Lying to Linda and Paul weighs heavily on David; he isn't deceitful by nature. I, too, hate the lies but the alternative is too horrible— telling Linda and Paul. I cannot contemplate it—I know, *know* that telling them will set off a chain of events that neither of us can anticipate or control. But David is burdened by the guilt and he wants to be rid of it; he can't see beyond that. And he did push—pushed me hard to commit myself to him by agreeing to tell Paul. Ultimately I was convinced, but I remained terrified, absolutely terrified of what I was about to do. Flying home, I couldn't swallow the honey-coated airplane peanuts, my mouth was so dry. "You know you're scared when your mouth is so dry that you can't spit," laughed my big-game hunter lover. I have never in my life been as afraid of what I was about to do—this despite having flown under enemy fire into Vietnamese and Laotian bases.

Sunday, December 8

Few things in my life will remain as crystal clear as the lonely half-hour drive from the county airport, dragging my suitcases out of the station wagon (How could I ask Paul to do that?), carrying them up to my two hundred-year-old farmhouse, opening the front door myself, shoving the heavy luggage through the opening, and looking up at Paul's joyful, welcoming face.

This is an image that will remain with me for the rest of my life. Paul took one look at my drained, white face and was filled with terror. He later said that he thought one of my parents had died. I said, "Let's sit down," and we did on the dark green sofa in the library. It's the room I most love in my home; the room with the big exposed logs, the wall filled with books, the large oak rolltop desk. It was the room I fantasized creating the first time I set foot in our aging, then unrenovated dream house six and a half years ago.

"I have to tell you something and this isn't going to be easy," I said. "I'm having an affair, have been having an affair for two months. It's serious. I'm in love." I went on, "I wasn't in Washington with Carol, I was in Boston with another man."

Paul's first reaction may have been relief: an affair, *this* he could handle, this he could wait out. He was consoling, loving, solicitous of *my* pain. But I kept at him, kept the image of David firmly in my mind. I didn't want Paul to think he could wait it out, I said; this was serious—I wouldn't be telling him it if were not. I wanted time, lots of time with my lover, I wanted it all— Paul to stand by me and time to explore the relationship with my lover. Then Paul asked who the man was. I hesitated. He asked, "Is it the man we are meeting tomorrow for dinner and a concert?" I said yes. He nodded as though to say, "Of course." And then he said, "I think this is where a drink is appropriate."

Paul seldom drinks and almost never in excess. He began drinking an entire bottle of Scotch. The night wore on. He sobbed, he called names, he said, "We should have never had a second child—this happened because we had a second child." I slept, he didn't. When I awakened, he was downstairs on the couch and he wanted to make love. My heart was so broken by what I was doing to him that I was about to acquiesce, but the children were up and I was relieved.

Nothing was resolved between Paul and me, nothing was clear-cut. I have no intention of relinquishing David, but neither am I ready to leave my marriage. Paul has given no ultimatums and I have made no promises.

David and I met, as planned, this afternoon. We met to compare notes, to take inventory of the damage to us and to our marriages. It wasn't an easy day. For the first time we were together with the full knowledge of my husband and his wife, and that cast a very different light on our meeting. Linda begged David not to come to me; David said he could not stay late. We wandered the streets of a small college town two hours from home, studiously avoiding private places—at least that's how it felt to me. Abruptly he began making future plans: the two of us moving to some obscure town on the Canadian border in upstate New York that he and Linda had explored last winter. The town had a lucrative practice he could slide into and a big Victorian house he loved. I simply gagged on his questions and his plans. I was choking, physically choking under his pressure. I was not ready to declare myself, to move, to answer his questions about my career needs. Jesus, David, I am choking!

We drove home, and on the way, I badly needed to just *hold* him. All this talk: Linda calling me "that Jewish bitch"; Linda warning David, "Inette is just after your money"; Linda instructing Dave, "Remember your responsibilities"; Linda threatening Dave, "If you do this to me, I'll pick your bones." All this talk—all the hurts and all the anger and Dave thrusting the future on me—I wanted and needed only to be held. For this purpose and at my insistence, we stopped for the first time at an actual motel, a roadside Holiday Inn. It was essential time spent looking deeply into each others' eyes and intentions. David said, "It is my intention to marry you." Maybe for the first time, I realized that David *is* putting it all on the line. While my head is filled to brimming with doubts about leaving Paul, my marriage, and all that is familiar, Dave takes the risks. His marriage, his family, his medical practice are all out there on the line for loving me. This was the first time I realized the degree of David's commitment; I'm also aware of the degree to which I have held back. So if I love this man—and I do—I must decide. Will I marry him or will I stay with Paul? It appears David will settle for no less. Hunter that he is, he tells me he wants the "clean shot." I am very much in love with him.

Monday, December 9
I put this letter into David's parked Jeep.

My dear, dear David,
I'm propped up in my bed, the bed you well know, leaning on my knees writing this. For the past three hours this room has been filled with family—beautiful children playing hard, my husband of many years building a fire here—allowing me to sleep late after a very tough night and then with very little encouragement bringing me breakfast in bed on the wicker tray he gave me last Christmas. He allowed me to hold his hands and tell him how good he looked in the red flannel shirt he bought on our last trip without kids in September.

David, I love you. You are right, you do not fill a void in my life. But what you have done is create a place, a niche—but much more enormous than a niche—of your own in my life. It's a place that in my wildest imaginings I can not imagine unfilled, vacant. Dave, yesterday with you was like daylight. All my self-deception fell aside. Your face—oh, my God—your face. You have given, you do give me so very, very much; and yesterday it was clarity you gave. How much more could I be loved? Those hours of enlightenment yesterday may or may not have had the effect on me you expected. I came home to a very sad-faced, calm, and conciliatory but deeply hurt Paul, sitting in the wicker bedroom chair staring. I knew I had to reach out to this man whom I *do* love, to really feel and see what it is I contemplate leaving. And I did. I tried to talk. He was reticent. He told me that his one ultimatum was that I could not say I loved him while I was with you. And he said that he never wanted me to come back to him because you sent me back—that it had to be my choice. Then I said, "Dave wants to marry me"; and Paul broke down, ran away, and said, "My God, it's been twenty-six hours since I've gone from being a man married for fifteen years to being told that my wife sleeps with another man, to being told that she loves him, and now that he wants to marry her— give me a break!"

And then there were harsh, silly words he instantly regretted. He talked about going to court on Linda's behalf, of having your medical license revoked.

We went to bed, at my bidding, here together in this bed and fell asleep. But sometime around three A.M. I awakened, instantly full of the light our hours together yesterday had shed on me, on you, on my life. And I started sobbing, sobbing like I've never ever sobbed in my life—cries yanked from my depths. And in the dark, as Paul held me, I told him all that I feel, told him as I could not the night before because I didn't know.

I told him that I have no doubts. I have no doubts about him or our marriage—that the usual way to disengage yourself emotionally from a marriage is to tear your spouse apart, criticize your marriage—but that I couldn't do that or feel that. I said, "I'm sure of all that's been here for all of these years."

But I told him that I'm equally certain of my love for you, yours for me, and what we are together. I said that two months sounds trivial next to fifteen years, but that it is not, *it is not.* I said I could not envision a resolution. How can I give up the one, how can I give up the other? And I sobbed. David, I talked and talked about you and me, about Paul and the kids, and I faced what I've been repressing these months (but what you have always seen clearly), and I sobbed and held Paul until he soothed me to sleep.

And this morning I knew I wanted to give them a chance— the them who've not had a chance these weeks or months. I cannot, Dave, contemplate leaving my family and marrying you now. I'm pretty sure of that. I'd like to emphasize the "now" and hold out hope for our future, but I don't really know, can't really know, and I realize your preference for "the clean shot." But having said this—having said that I cannot leave them— please, please please don't make me give you up, give up what we have now. Paul is convinced that our affair will go on a long, long time. He is prepared for the long haul, though he tells me that things can never be the same. David, that is what *I* want now. I want to see you, be with you every possible moment, to build a future slowly together until there is an inevitability one way or the other.

I cannot, *cannot* imagine my life without yours being a part of it. I cannot give us up. I cannot be away from your eyes. Now, I also remember what you said last night, though I'm working hard at fudging on the exact memory. I fear that you said something like, "all or nothing." I know that you have, as you said, "put all your cookies on the table."

If I felt, as I fear, that this letter would precipitate the end of us, I'm certain I'd tear it up right now. And yet, of course, how can I? We have been nothing but truthful with each other.

So, I want to argue that what I'm writing changes nothing—

except, perhaps, the degree of your hope—and maybe that is everything. But I want to argue that you have always known the degree of my marital pull, even when I have not. How often have you said, "*You*, Inette, have a genuinely good marriage, but I only have the quote good end quote marriage?" So what I'm saying is just a recognition and confirmation of the realities that have always existed. But, oh, my God, I do fear that you will read this otherwise and demand that I relinquish what I cannot relinquish and go on breathing.

If Paul and the kids are my ballast, my heart, my comfort, you, David are the great and enduring love of my life—the spirit, the possibility, the hope, the dreams, the soul within my soul. Please, please, please, Dave, stay with me.

>All the love of which I am capable—and that
>is great indeed,

>>>Inette

I think it's essential to say one last thing here. This letter confessing to the pull of my marriage is not a confession of loving you less, Dave. I've never loved you more than I have since last night. Your face is no longer difficult to conjure when I'm with Paul. It's now always right in front of my eyes. I have never loved you more in all ways. I realize this letter does not read like a love letter. Perhaps the next one will.

>>>I

Tuesday, December 10

This was a most difficult and painful day. Very early this morning, the phone rang. I answered, and it was David's voice saying, "Inette, I want to speak to Paul." Instantly I realized that Dave had read the letter I'd put in his Jeep yesterday and was about to do the only thing he could do—end us. Being the honorable man he is, he was facing up to my husband. "David, don't do this to me," I begged. He replied, "I've written you a letter, Inette, let me speak to Paul." And he did.

My description of what transpired comes from Paul. David told him he would never again see me. My husband described my lover as "tortured by guilt," a guilt very familiar to my Catholic husband. "What religion is he, anyway?" Paul asked. David once described himself as "a variation on the Paul theme," and in this phone conversation, the part that was familiar to each of them in the other man was apparent. My husband walked away believing David was an honorable and decent man. My lover walked away, I later learned, relieved that Paul had treated him to no hostility or nastiness—another gentleman. They each understood, respected, and even liked each other.

I felt impotent. I felt acted upon, without recourse, and angry. I stormed around, I paced the room, I ran the thirty-five farm acres, I felt trapped in my dream home. I needed to talk to David again; I needed a last meeting—a real good-bye. I knew David wouldn't accept my call at his office, so I did the only thing I could do: I begged my husband to call my lover and plead my case for one last meeting, one last Wednesday.

I realized the full weight of the cruelty of asking Paul to call David. But I could not do otherwise. I had to see David again. All Paul's instincts told him to not give in to me on this one. All his sound judgment said, "No, I will not call." But I persisted, and he said, "Take some time, think about this for a couple of hours. If you still want it, I'll call." And he did. "Ultimately only your words will allow Inette to accept the end," he said to David.

What Paul didn't count on, what I dared not hope for, were the effect of my words on Dave and his on me: *"Please see me one last time." "Of course, Inette."* And then there followed an endless stream of words, vacillation, and more words. Paul sat on the stairs, head in hand, while the phone call continued longer than expected. "I was planning the victory celebration before the game was played," my college-football-player husband said. "Up until now I have followed my instincts; in calling David for you, I have gone against them."

Wednesday, December 11

We met at the hospital, and because it was the last time, we climbed into my station wagon and drove off together through town. Secrecy no longer seemed necessary.

We arrived at the Country Inn and they knew us, had the champagne bucket filled with ice and waiting. We retreated. Next Monday is David's thirty-ninth birthday. I had put together an odd and sentimental gift: a collection of sequential photographs from my childhood to the present in an album with lots of pages left for our own photographic story to unravel. I'd gone to considerable effort and expense to have these old photos reproduced in uniform size and in black and white. I'd written descriptive captions on each page, and I've been thrilled in anticipation of David's reaction. He is such a sentimentalist. But now we wouldn't be together on David's birthday, so with a heavy heart I gave him my present today.

David cried, good serious crying. Unlike Paul, he is *not* a man who cries. "I haven't cried since I was five years old," he said. "No one has ever given me a better present." He cried and he looked so open and vulnerable and I wanted only to hold him very tight.

And again we felt a need to be together, to make a life together. I asked David to give it his best shot, to woo me and seduce me and overpower me with the extent and depth of his love—to convince me that I could, in fact, leave Paul. In every way, this reserved man opened himself to me and loved me. I tried to match his love and, ultimately, his commitment. "I will go home and tell Linda that I cannot give you up," he said, then he asked, "What will you tell Paul?" And I clutched, panicked. The picture of Paul's face filled my head and the pain that picture evinced involuntarily contorted my face. In a flash, David saw that I could not tell Paul. The drive home was not easy. Nothing was resolved, but I guess, everything was. This was our last meeting.

Thursday, December 12
I told David I would send Linda a letter, and today I did.

Dear Linda,
I've just written one last letter to Dave—it followed one last phone call, which followed yesterday's last time together. I feel compelled to write you, uncertain as I am just what it is I want to say to you.

I do want to say I am sorry—so sorry for the hurt and the pain and the deceit I've contributed to. Sorry for any doubts I've planted in your head and heart. And in saying that weak word, *sorry*, I realize how little that expresses of what I feel.

I realize the anger, hostility—hatred, perhaps—you feel toward me and I understand and accept that. I realize you may feel my words are filled with hypocrisy and I've earned that, too. It was neither my goal nor my intention to harm your marriage, but I acted consistently with self-interest.

Linda, ultimately what I want to say to you is that your abiding love of David, your fifteen-year marriage, the family and life you've built together won out. Ultimately, faced with choices, Dave chose what you and he have together. And, with a full heart, I can say that is right and as it should be.

I have no personal regrets. I loved David as honestly and fully as I was able. In my brief moment, I felt I'd found the world— glory, the light, a very deep happiness. I cannot regret this.

I do sorrow for the hurts to you and, of course, to Paul. But I have an abiding faith that from all the hurts, the pain, there will arise for you and Dave, for Paul and me, a renewed commitment, a deeper love.

Please accept my thoughts and feelings as absolutely sincere without motive for gain.

                                        Inette

Friday, December 13
Now I know—*now*—I know why you don't have love affairs. I am so leaden, so empty, so hollow, so hopeless.

After our resolve to end it, David called four times. The first call affirmed the end, the second call salved the wounds, the third call interrupted Paul's and my shaky effort at reconciliation, the fourth was desperation and I requested no more calls.

Yesterday, I felt trapped in my own home, caged in this place I used to love.

I confided to my brother by phone today the story of this affair. He and his daughters visited here Thanksgiving, and he sensed then that something was very wrong. We had long private talks over that holiday visit, but I skirted the actual fact that I was involved with a man. Today on the phone, he said, "I doubt this is the end." I answered, "Don't say that!" "These things don't end so easily," he said. And now—already—I understand. How can I never again know the highs? Even when David calls, my blood races and my energy surges. I feel briefly alive. And then the deadness settles in. I can't imagine that I'll ever again be happy.

Yet I know starting up again is impossible, deadly—a diminishing of what we've been. Already, talking to my brother and my friend Anna puts David and me into the category "people who have affairs"—a generic type, an academic classification.

So I am trapped. Can I return to him knowing we're doomed to snatch a few wonderful moments and destroy the rest? Or do I stay with our resolve and feel lifeless, hopeless, without the spark of my love? The very fact that I'm again writing in a journal instead of writing to David is a horrible confirmation of the change. I want to write to *him*.

Later in the day

It goes on. I've been getting the boys Christmas haircuts, showing them the decorations at the hotel. I can't cope. I'm on the brink of a major embarrassing scene at all times. I need to be institutionalized, strapped to a bed, and filled with drugs. I can't deal with any aspect of my life. I need, *need* to hear David's voice—I so regret telling him not to call. I've made a major mess of my life, my marriage, my family, my Dave. I seem to have no stabilizing resources of my own. I've never been so lost. I've really screwed up and there's no one to blame. David blames himself for my pain. I don't blame myself for his—how dare he presume!

I talk at Paul, he mostly listens. I need to talk or to write in order to keep hanging on. This all feels so self-destructive—I've never before been self-destructive.

How is David doing? God, I want him to feel this pain. I'm so jealous that he has his work, his constant work to divert him. Yet he hates my pain, my pain pains him—I really am unworthy.

I'm realizing here how little I have going in my life right now. All these years of intensive child rearing, and now I look to David to lift me out of the morass. Is that right? Is that as it should be? What do I present to Dave—a woman begging to be defined by him but petrified of letting a mere man define her?

The analogy to drug withdrawal is apt.

Tuesday, December 17

For three solid days, until this morning when he went to work, I haven't been five feet away from Paul. I've been hanging on for dear life. I've been telling him the intimate details of what I feel for David constantly, in an effort to distance David and rebuild Paul and me. He's listened with enormous love and patience. He knows the nature of my pain. He knows because I tell him that I don't think I can make it without Dave. For three days, I've talked and cried about David—and all the while clinging for dear life to Paul, the only hope, if there is any hope of making it through this separation.

My reaching out to Paul makes starkly clear the damage done to our marriage. There is about me, in my reaching out, desperation and fear. There is from Paul great forced compassion and love. He knows that if he lets up for one moment, I will flee. I know that if I let up for a minute, I'll become aware of what I've given up in David and go crazy. We both know that it can't continue like this. Paul hopes that each day I'll grow stronger, that time is our ally. I have less faith that I'm growing stronger—it stays the same.

Last Friday, Paul predicted that within three weeks I'd accept what David and I decided as the only way—that further relations between us would only cause further pain. I don't know if he really believes it or he's intent on talking me through this like an alcoholic at AA.

Later in the day

There among the Christmas cards, tucked inside my blue rural mailbox at the end of the gravel and rock driveway, was a letter from David. A last letter. There was about the letter a sad, sad finality. There seemed to be an ease for David in that finality— a palpable relief—a contentment to live his life as he has, with just the added spice of memories of Dave and Inette. Then he enclosed a photo of himself. It's touching that he remembered my request for one, but peculiar, nonetheless. Peculiar, because I remember seeing that picture at the Muller's dinner party just three days before I sent my initial note inviting him to bed. And I remember, clearly remember, being wildly attracted to Dave in that photo—my heart actually fluttered at the jaunty picture of him under that safari hat. Now, however, when I look at this same photograph, I cannot see *enough* of him in the shadow of that hat. It's the perfect metaphor, but immensely frustrating that I can't get enough: enough of his hair, his eyes, his face, his smile, his dimple. It's as though he's hiding behind the corpse of that zebra.

I think of all the words people have spoken to me. My brother saying: "What David doesn't know about you is that you don't make demands of Inette or she will turn 180 degrees and head off in the other direction." Is that what I've done with David? As he tightened the screws, did I spite myself in reaction? Friend Anna is the only other person I've confided in these past days. David has told no one but Linda (he's a very private person), Paul has told no one, and Linda lives in terror that someone may find out. But I needed to talk, and my brother Greg (whose wife left him) and my friend Anna (who left her first husband for her second) seemed likely choices and safely distant from here—he's in Baltimore, she's in Chapel Hill.

Anna said, "His timetable isn't yours. When the time is right, something inside of you clicks." Is it coincidental that the moment David backed off, no longer demanded me on his terms, that I could see my way clear? I've always felt I needed a little space, when push came to shove. But I hated to ask it, because *he* was so willing to take the risks.

Thursday, December 19

Paul has pulled out the heavy artillery. He's given up trying to convince me what I'm giving up in our marriage. Instead he took another tactic. He undermined my confidence in David's love and need for me. He insisted that I face the reality—David has excised me from his life and he feels relief that the guilt is over. "Why did he press you so hard," asked Paul, "if he didn't want the affair to end?" For hours Paul lectured me, and I cried and yelled back at him. "Call him," Paul finally shouted. "Call him and humiliate yourself. Find out David doesn't want you." He was very convincing. I feel strengthened in my resolve.

Friday, December 20

Today, late this afternoon, nine days after I'd last seen him and a week beyond our final phone conversation, David called. I'd gotten through his birthday, through the Tuesday at noon without his usual call, through the first Wednesday afternoon without Dave, through minutes and hours and now days of intense loneliness.

"Inette, it's Dave." I was shocked and absolutely silent. Then I said, "Your timing stinks." He asked, "Would you rather I not call?" I said, "Oh, my God, *no*. I need to hear from you."

"I know it's pathetic," he said, "but I'd settle for talking to you for five minutes, once a month." I answered, "Not pathetic, just unrealistic."

Saturday, December 21
I left this letter in David's Jeep.

My dear David,
Last night at a party at the Ullman's, I wore my pearls and thought of you. Last night, on the drive to the party through the snow, Paul talked about necessary changes we must make in our lives to improve it—moves, jobs, intellectual stimulation— and I thought of you.

I arrived at the party, and the very first person I saw was Abby. Her first words were, "I saw David Muller and I met his wife last Saturday." (No, she isn't suspicious, only envious that *we* have a social relatonship with you.) Then Abby went on—and on— and on about how good you looked, how much weight you'd lost, how warm and friendly you were. She related all the details of the doctors' dance—and for the duration of a rather slow party, I thought of you.

You tell me a five-minute phone call once a month is ac- ceptable to you, Dave. Well, here's what is clear to me. Your five-minute phone call is great when there's nothing else. Then I'll need your fifteen-minute phone call—and that will work for about twelve hours. Then I'll need a letter—which will hold me for as much as a day. And then I'll need to see you. And when I see you, I almost immediately will need to see you again. And the fact is, David, that I already know I'll need to hold you, kiss you, and feel you next to me. I already know that any frequency we schedule won't be enough. I draw absolutely no conclusions from what I've just said, but, David, these are the facts.

When I told you yesterday, "We have boxed ourselves in," you responded, "Oh, I don't know about that. I intend to live a long, long time." I haven't been able to get that out of my mind. Your continued commitment means everything to me.

I think a lot about our last Wednesday together—your tears when I gave you the birthday present; your wonderful laughter when they led us to that huge three-bedroom suite and I said, "We should have brought the kids."

What I *do* know is that the moment I'm with you again, all of this—all the memories I've suppressed so as not to feel the pain and the feelings and the reality of you—will come rushing at me with gale force and bowl me over. This I know as surely as I breathe, as surely as I attend the circuit of Christmas parties and smile and flirt and publicly hug my husband—this I know.

And so this Christmas week apart is, for me, just buying a little more time, and I'm not even sure for what. But I guess it's a way of delaying something that seems more and more inevitable. I'm grateful, very grateful for the leeway you're giving me and us now. I'm eternally grateful for your patience, your love, your open door.

I love you,
Inette

Monday, December 23

I'm uncertain how it happened. Paul was planning a romantic evening for just the two of us. It sounded good to me. After all, this resolution to continue the enforced separation another week was a way to reach out to Paul. I'm genuinely unsure how it happened—how it is that I wanted to call David, to hear his voice. I asked Paul to permit it, and he did. David, it turns out, was free this evening. Paul, in some weird twist of mind, suggested then insisted that I go see David. Of course, it was some kind of test. I knew that and I failed it. I seized the opportunity to see Dave.

I drove to David's office early this evening. The clinic was closed. It was now almost two weeks since our last meeting. My blood pounded my veins and I was very scared, but excited, as I drove to his office.

My God, there he was. There was that incredibly beautiful face, and then we hugged—shoulder-to-shoulder, a physical fit very different than mine with the much larger Paul. It felt like a miracle to be in this man's arms again, to touch his face, his hair, to have him revel in my unruly natural curls. It didn't seem possible—after all the horrible pain, the loneliness, the fears—

that we were here together again. It was unquestionably right.

This was the neutral meeting ground I wanted. There wasn't even a couch in his office. I sat down in a vinyl office chair; David was in the other. (The exact same chairs, in fact, that Paul and I first sat in—me newly pregnant and meeting my obstetrician—six years ago). I clutched my four pages of written challenges and objections to a future with David Muller. Throughout the two-week separation, I added carefully numbered challenges on the yellow legal pad. They now numbered thirty— thirty good, serious reasons why David and I didn't belong to- gether over the long haul. Some of the reasons were Paul's, some my brother's, some Anna's, some my own. I read David the list, slowly, point by point, and he listened solemnly. At the end, he looked me straight in the eye and said, "Piece of cake." I was elated.

For the first time in almost sixteen years, I removed my wed- ding band from my finger and David did the same. The wedding bands were identical, plain gold rings, and we set them on his desk and held each other. When I left—with a very stiff neck from the contortions in the straight-back chairs—I knew I was committed. There was no way I could give up David.

Paul had typed out his thoughts while I was gone and, on impulse, scrawled my name on the top, with his on the bottom. Before he went to bed, he left the typed sheet for me to read on the hall table.

There have been many strange days since that Saturday night when she came with "the news." In fact, each of them in their own way has had a weird twist or two, an unexpected turn of emotion or reaction or insight, yet today must be the strangest. I virtually pushed her out the door into the arms of her lover, precisely the opposite behavior of what I have been advocating. I encouraged her to call him. I manufactured an opportunity for them to be together, at night, when passions notoriously run high.

I drank my Scotch and smoked my dollar cigar alone, of

course. She was in the night, perhaps to him by now, fumbling among their winter coats to grasp the forms beneath. I allowed it—in so many words, I gave my permission.

I know why I have done this, but I cannot put it into words. Rather I know a few reasons why I did it and I cannot decide which one is the real one. Knowing the way the world works, I probably did it for every reason I can think of.

We had planned an intimate evening. I had proposed hopping into bed the minute the kids were asleep. I planned an out-loud reading of some sophisticated erotica and the delights of intense love making. We needed to feel close again, to touch one another below the façade of repression. We planned to light the fire and heat the room against the cold of a December night. We would talk between the accumulating moans; we would feel the closeness we need. But I pushed her out the door to God-knows-what delights with him.

I am not quite the victim I seem; I hope they will fight. But who knows, perhaps I delude myself again, and they will indeed fight but come closer together in the process of making up. Every action has so far had an unpredictable reaction—it would only be appropriate if this would in fact occur. Maybe I am the victim, the classic victim, the one you read about somewhere. Maybe I will end up months down the road much like I am now, drinking Scotch, smoking a cheaper cigar and alone. Maybe their love will win out, and I will be left with a cheap fantasy of intimate love on a Monday night in December. Maybe the dice rolled to their fated positions long before that night she came home and told me she was having an affair with a man I knew socially. Maybe one love must die when another one begins, and maybe that is the law of the universe I hadn't known until now. Maybe none of us knew.

She wanted to fuck and run, but you can't do that. That's another law of the universe at least she learned and I suspected. Orgasms produce bonds that cannot be denied. Does he like to fuck first and talk later, as I did at one time? Now I like to talk and fuck at the same time. She fucked him and stayed around to talk. I know she put her diaphragm in before she left or at least seriously thought about it as she dressed for him, down to the ultimate detail.

I pushed her out the door. I participated fully in the affair. I condone the fucking. I gave her him instead of me.

So I'll let them make the mistakes this time. I don't seem to have made many, and yet to no real avail; every now and then it hits me how truly irrelevant my actions just might be. So maybe it's time to adopt a give-them-enough-rope attitude.

She said she loved me. She said she loved me and him, too. I thought I had to win in the long run since the roots of our love go so far back into the mists—to college students away for the year and growing up—and they all lead to now. To now, when she is away, away with the one she says she loves now and loves even more desperately than she can admit. They all lead to now, and God knows what future they lead to when I cannot even manage a future of one night after the other without her longings for him coming between us.

She chooses to spend her time with him, time she could choose to spend with me,—she's on the telephone, and she's on the road to their secret meeting place and to the place where he lies to his wife, but we agree to the journey because we don't know what else to do.

Saturday, December 28

My parents visited here Christmas week. Paul and I tried hard to keep up the veneer of normality. We went through all the Christmas rituals—trekking up the mountain to cut the tree (perhaps symbolically choosing one that was bent, kept falling over, and had to be tied up to the wall). Fifteen-year-old ornaments smashed to the ground in one fall. Everyone, everywhere seemed euphoric, and it was oppressive. Paul and I refused to make New Year's plans—we had no resources left after Christmas.

Christmas Day was the last day Paul and I made love. I didn't want to because of my increasing loyalty to David. But Paul was so entreating, so genuine, so full of love and desire for me, so appealing in his own right. In the middle of the afternoon, Christmas Day, with the children napping and my parents downstairs, we retreated to our bedroom and made love. As always, our love making was lovely and fine, but I was filled with ambivalence. Afterward I lay in bed thinking of David. Paul felt my thoughts wander. "This, Inette, is why you can't have an affair and a marriage," he said. "Because in that woozy twilight period after sex, when you can't control the direction of your thoughts, I know your thinking of David and that hurts—that intrudes on our love."

Last night was a night of extraordinary violence. Paul didn't touch me, but the verbal abuse was extreme. He was drinking, then drinking some more. He smashed glasses against the woodstove hearth; he threw a half-full bottle of bourbon at the stove and started a fire; he tore off his pajama bottoms and shoved them into the fire. So the entire angry scene took place bottomless—again, symbolic of his sexual rage. Our son Max whimpered upstairs in his bedroom, listening and afraid of the abuse his father heaped on me and fearing, I later learned, that his father—the gentlest of men—would harm me. Paul did loom huge. His physical strength appeared enormous, his ability to find my most vulnerable underside honed to perfection. The obscenities and the description of my life, my person, my values, were all hurled with enormous venom and hatred.

This morning at breakfast, I was terrified of Paul and his destructive possibilities. There had been hours of rage. Paul was conciliatory, frightened himself of the rage he still felt. He had no recollection of the specifics, but there were scattered shards of glass and upended furniture to remind him. He called a psychologist friend, Eleanor, and immediately began crisis counseling.

Sunday, December 29

I did a very unexpected and maybe unforgivable thing this morning. With neither prior planning nor forethought, I felt moved to call Linda Muller. I think of this woman I have known socially for a year as another woman in pain—and I assume responsibility for some of her pain. She isn't a woman whom, by nature, I identify with or would choose as a friend—but she is another woman and my feminist consciousness rebels at what I do to her. I guess all the above contributed to my impulse to phone Linda. We spoke at some length.

I asked to see her. She adamantly refused. "I do not know why I'm calling you, Linda," I said—and it was true—"but I think we're becoming caricatures of ourselves to one another and that it's important to remember the real person." I felt some need to reach out and talk. "Sure, you want to talk," Linda spat at me. "You're a good talker, that's what you do best." She accused me of feigning interest in her friendship to seduce her husband, of using her. And I guess that must be true. "I'm not proud of that," I said. She told me that I was in for a big surprise—that David was "an empty hollow man with no beliefs." She insisted that I was attracted only by his good looks and his money.

"Money isn't an issue," I answered. "My parents have it." She hissed, "Well, mine didn't, but they were rich in love." "Mine, too," I whispered. "Then you had it all, didn't you?" she screamed.

I talked about how none of this was easy, how the pain and suffering was intense for all four of us, how I hated what I was doing to Paul and that the thought of the children's suffering was excruciating. I cried as I talked and Linda listened for a while, but then, finding herself listening, she attacked with steely anger. "I don't know what you and David think you have, but it sure isn't love. I don't know what it is—you know how to flatter him, to feed his ego, to make him feel like a big man.

Please never call here again." And I answered, "I won't Linda,
I'm sorry."

After the call, I was shaking. What exactly had I hoped to
accomplish? I seem to have this tremendous urge to do exactly
as I please with David and I still want Paul and Linda to accept
it without rancor. I keep saying things to Paul about our being
decent to each other. But, of course, being decent to me is in
neither Paul's nor Linda's best interest.

Monday, December 30

This morning Paul made a major miscalculation. As we lay
in bed together, with the bright winter sun pouring onto our
canopy bed, he gave me an ultimatum. The ultimatum was clearly
fueled by yesterday's session with the psychologist Eleanor. "Inette,"
he said, "I can no longer allow this affair to continue. You must
give it up, or we must separate." And in a split second, without
a moment's hesitation, I answered, "You're right. We must separate." He was stunned—the wind was knocked out of his sails.
But the fact is, I can no longer live with Paul, sleep in his bed,
and plan to build a life with David. I can no longer live with
myself, living like this.

I was summoned to speak with Eleanor, formerly our friend
and now Paul's therapist. She wanted to know my intentions.
"I don't want marriage counseling. I want only to be with David,"
I said. Then separation was essential, she said—but it must be
completely on Paul's timetable. I was not to leave until he ordered
me out. Further, she insisted I must be the one to move out.
Paul must be left in the familiarity of our home.

I want the separation, but I had hoped Paul would move out.
I'm petrified to leave my home of six years. Nevertheless, I
accepted Eleanor's conditions. It seemed the least I could do.

At this point, when my marriage of almost sixteen years is
about to be sacrificed, little more than two months have passed
since Dave and I first met at the Country Inn. The speed and
intensity of our love has been awesome. "Two Type-A's making
sparks," is what Paul calls us, and there's something to that. The

breathtaking acceleration of our affair shocks even us. The unanimous considered response to the pair of us is, "Go slow, slow down," but it's spitting in the wind. We can't go slow. There's something in the chemistry of David and Inette that drives each of us—and, of course, that's a large part of the attraction.

Wednesday, January 1, 1986

Last night—New Year's Eve, 1985/1986—was disastrous. Paul had a hidden agenda. He came home from work full of bustling plans and surprises. He put the children to bed early, lit the library fire, filled the room with candles, cleared a dance floor behind the sofa, put Mel Torme on the stereo, and broke out a bottle of champagne and exquisite handmade chocolates. I got increasingly nervous and I said, "This isn't going to end in bed is it?" "Trust me," he answered. "I know all these awful things are going on in our lives, but tonight is New Year's, and let's just forget all the rest and dance and watch the fire and talk." I said, "Okay, let's do that."

But that's not how it went. Paul's sexual intentions were revealed when I happened upon my diaphragm, which he'd put in a desk drawer. I panicked. I could no longer betray David by making love to Paul—a peculiar twist, I realize—but my own form of morality, if you will. I chose my words carefully, "I can't make love to you, Paul, because my fidelity has shifted to David." And with that, Paul went crazy—spewing rage, venom, orders to leave our home immediately. I refused to leave without a separation agreement (I feared my leaving would jeopardize future custody of the children). There was more anger and Paul retreated alone to our bedroom.

At eleven P.M. on New Year's Eve, I called a friend who is an attorney and everything changed color. The high emotions were about to be transformed into legal documents and it felt awful.

Part III
ENTRENCHED

Monday, January 6

David and I took a long-planned weekend away in Asheville. It was the calm in the eye of the storm. We had a long, leisurely Sunday breakfast in an elegant old hotel dining room, making plans and touching souls. It was just two days, but it felt removed and expandable. Asheville is about all that's right between David and I—it's about feeling loved and cherished, believing everything is possible. If Boston was the acknowledgement of the inevitable, Asheville is the unhurried planning for that inevitable. Dave drove from Asheville straight to his home, loaded his Jeep with clothing and hunting gear, and drove to his friend and colleague's home to ask for shelter. He told Linda he was moving out.

Paul had planned to confide in several selected good local friends while I was away. He was to search for support and comfort. It seemed to make sense. But I hadn't anticipated the results of going public with our private pain. Everything has dramatically changed, now that the details of our lives are exposed to the prying eyes of other people. I came home from

Asheville not just to Paul and the kids, but to a good, old male friend encamped in my house, who refused to utter a word to me, refused to leave my home when asked, refused to give Paul and me a moment alone. There was a verbal brawl, and it shook me.

I telephoned two women friends Paul had confided in. The first said, "You're no longer my friend. All the values and assumptions we shared are no longer there. You betrayed me. You won't want to live in Watertown. You will be ostracized. No one will speak to you." The second woman, Ellen, had left her husband of ten years for another man. She said, "What do you want from me? What you're doing bears no similarity to what I did. You're being cruel and thoughtless. It took me nine years to extricate myself from an abusive marriage. You'll regret this every day of your life. You *think* you have felt pain, but you haven't even begun to feel pain."

Tuesday, January 7

Paul and I have been bearing the overwhelming weight of having to tell the children—our happy, loving, lighthearted children—that we're going to separate. We are both filled with dread. There's no better father than Paul—in every way, he's a nurturing, involved, active parent. The parental roles in our family are so blurred that Max still occasionally calls me "Daddy" and Paul "Mommy" before he corrects himself. He's always used the words interchangeably. What do two bookish people do when faced with emotional crisis? They consult a book, of course. Paul brought one home that detailed how to tell your child you're about to separate. We followed the advice.

It said: Max, age five, and Andrew, age two, must be together; both parents must be present. We were told to rehearse what we intended to say so there'd be no push and pull. We agreed that I would talk first; there would be no recriminations. We have always been and continue to be good parents.

"Parents can't divorce children," I said. "We will both always love you and take care of you." We talked for a half-hour.

Andrew said nothing, but he did listen. Max asked questions about logistics: "Where will Daddy live? Where will Mommy live? Where will me and Andrew live?" At first Max laughed— the same immediate nervous reaction he had when his puppy was hit by a truck and killed. Then he grew solemn, listened intently, and finally wanted to hear no more. "I don't want to talk any more." Several hours later Max approached me with a big grin, "Mommy," he pronounced, "I think you're going to change your mind before you marry David."

Wednesday, January 8

Today, I rented the first apartment I looked at. I walked into a clean, bright, two-bedroom place; looked around; and had an impossible time imagining myself in this town apartment after six years in the country. It looked nice enough, but I had absolutely no way of knowing if it would be adequate, appropriate to my needs—me in an apartment with two kids? It was mind boggling. So I flipped a coin and told the landlord that I would take it, mostly because I couldn't prolong the exhaustion of the search. I've probably made the quickest decision of my life. It takes me longer to buy a pair of shoes.

The details: Paul ordered me out of our home on New Year's Day, so I'm free of the promise his therapist extracted that I stay until he tells me to leave. Yet he is filled with remorse. On the advice of my lawyer, Sherry, I've drawn up a separation agreement, since she hopes that Paul will agree to a no-fault divorce and avoid an ugly contested one. But Paul occasionally speaks with venom of dragging me through the courts on charges of "adultery" and fighting for custody of the children. David is taking the more direct route—he is filing for divorce, and Linda will be served by the county sheriff.

The logistics: I found the apartment, I'll furnish it, and all the utilities will be in my name. David will live here with the children and me, and he'll pay the rent. He's been out of his house, staying at the home of a doctor friend since Sunday.

Alone in this town that's David's, not mine, I had to search for a telephone to make the necessary calls to electric, phone, and water hook-ups, for garbage collection. How many years have passed since I've last made these kinds of transients' phone calls? I once thrived on being transient—a move a year for twelve years and then this long stretch in the country. Of course, I know what to do, but it all feels so much harder than it used to—than it should.

This note awaited my return home.

Inette,

All I was saying last night is that you owe it to yourself—you must do this for your own self-respect—to examine very seriously just what it is you are doing to yourself, to me, to David. You must talk to yourself (not to me, not to David, not to your mother) in the most blunt, direct, straightforward, honest way possible, as you have never done before in your life. You are about to take the most important step of your life (no, you haven't taken it yet) and therefore to do anything less would simply be shameful. If that means praying, if it means talking to a therapist of some sort, if it means staring into a cup of coffee in a diner, if it means standing in a meadow and screaming, you have to do it. I refuse to let you walk out the door without doing this. You are too important to me.

Paul

Friday, January 10

Moving day, my mother's birthday. There really isn't much to write here. I'm numb and very tired, just trying to cope with two small children and their energy in a very small apartment (children for whom thirty-five acres is a back yard).

Paul left the house with Andrew early to avoid the whole moving scene. The moving van came. Strangers packed my life into a truck—no, it was half my life, the half of my choosing. The rest still sits in the farmhouse of my dreams. The selected furniture and boxes paraded past me, revealing huge dust balls and small children's toys scattered unreachably under sofas—

now exposed. Everything looked dirty and I futilely swept room after room and picked up things off the floor. Ultimately, the dining room was completely empty, the guest bed gone from Andrew's room, the sofa from the library, the wing chair from the living room, the curtains from several windows, the oriental rugs from everywhere, the hanging light from over the kitchen table. Max's room was intentionally left intact. My bedroom—now Paul's—was also virtually untouched. I sat looking at the empty spaces and the disarray and wrote Paul a good-bye note. Max raced around, thrilled to be helping with the move.

Now I'm here in this town—the movers have gone—it's an instant home. I'm very very scared. David is working. He will move in tomorrow.

Tuesday, January 14

I'm a different person, an entirely different person from who I was when I began this journal. Then I was filled with enthusiasms and hopes. Now I'm without the comforts of my two hundred-year-old farmhouse (my home of six years), without the familiarity of Paul (my love of nineteen years), without the children (I have to call Max to find out how school went instead of searching his book bag with him when he steps off the bus). We now share two children—three and a half days there and three and a half days here—half a week with their father, half a week with their mother. There's none of the peace and solitude of the country: the privacy, the quiet, the choosing when to engage the world.

I'm in an apartment in Watertown. I have moved my belongings and physically settled in. But everything is strange and uprooted. I've wanted and needed change, but I'm completely severed from everything I've known. Paul is at the farm, I am here. The children are shuffled back and forth—dislocated in this town apartment, missing me at their farm home. There are noises and neighbors and curtains that must be drawn after six years of none of that. I hear neighboring water pipes, slamming car doors, traffic on the road, and people who intrude themselves into my solitude.

And there is David, a man who thinks bagels for breakfast are exotic, a man whose food tastes are unknown when I grocery shop. He is himself cast out from all that's familiar. His happiness is still contagious—his conviction is still, to a large degree, my conviction. But he goes off to work day and night—and the first real understanding of his hours dawns on me. He's trying very hard to attend to me. But I'm ultimately alone here, though alone is better than when the kids are here and I try to fit them into this strange and disoriented life. I've filled these five days since the move with domestic trivia: furniture, groceries, trying ridiculously hard to build a nest. And I guess it's comfortable—always comfortable when David is here, sometimes comfortable when I'm alone, much less so when the children are here without their usual resources.

I'm intensely alone because I've been totally and completely isolated from my close local friends, severed from all friendship. The weekend in Asheville was the turning point. The three friends Paul told about the affair were empowered to tell others, and they did so with a vengeance. This is a very small community, and though the Mullers' circle of friends is not ours, the connections were made. The stories that circulate are full of guesswork and inaccuracies. Paul tells his story to anyone who will listen, Linda selectively tells her story, but David and I speak only to each other.

I've heard not one word of empathy, not one good wish, not one pat on the back. I'm perceived as the villain—destroying a good, gentle, sensitive, supportive husband and depriving him of the children he adores. In moving from a town of five hundred to a town of three thousand and openly living with the man who has delivered half the babies born here these past six years, I'm visible and I'm scandalous in a way I could never be in an urban area in 1986. I wear a scarlet letter. I say hello to women in stores, and they turn their backs and walk out. People look at me and see someone quite other than me. Straight, rigid, moral-beyond-reproach Inette—a scarlet woman? I look over my shoulder to see who it is they are seeing—it can't be me. David and I are the central topic of social conversation in a two-county area.

My good friends feel very threatened. The public consensus remains that Paul and I had the perfect marriage. I'm to blame for that consensus—I've done outstanding PR over the years. "If this is happening to Paul and Inette," goes the thinking, "this can happen to me." So my friends feel undermined and hate me for undermining them. More distant people are simply outraged by the scandal. Compassion is poured onto Paul and the children—they are wined and dined. But is there nothing left for me?

When my very close friend Ellen demanded, "What do you want from me?" I pitifully answered, "Just to be my friend." An archliberal friend queried, "How can you love someone who hunts big game in Africa?" A woman with whom I shared a book discussion club membership for nine months—and little else—called Linda Muller (with whom she had no relationship), identified herself as "Inette's very close friend," and proceeded to tell Linda, "Inette is after David's money. . . . She always wanted to marry a doctor. . . . She's not really very smart. . . . She's a flash in the pan, with no style at all." Mary, the simple country woman who babysat for both my children from infancy wrote:

> Inette, I personally don't believe in things like this, especially where small children are involved. I can't understand why a friend with beautiful children, a working husband, home, and everything going for you would just leave it. . . . Please make arrangements for Andrew, I just can't keep him. . . . It bothers me too much.

It's been weeks since I've spoken to my parents. At some point in late December, Paul in his anger took it upon himself to recruit them to his cause. I hadn't known he'd spoken to them, so their shocked and hostile phone call to me hours later simply floored me. I've not spoken to them since.

During my final week at the farm, I received a two A.M. phone call from Linda Muller, frantically searching for her husband who had already moved out. "I'm going to come down to your farm and kill you," she said. And it occurred to me that she very well might. When I moved here, I had my new phone number unlisted. That ensures and completes my isolation.

Only Anna and Martin Farley, who met and married under circumstances similar to Dave's and mine, remain neutral. No one else asks to hear my story or asks how I feel. I'm alone as I've never in my life been alone. Friends have always been essential to me. Where, before, David's differences were wonderfully exciting, now cast out on my own with no home or husband or friends to draw on, it's all very frightening.

David, meanwhile, encounters only support and encouragement for his move. There was a public perception of the inadequacy of Dave and Linda's marriage—a realization that shocks David. Colleagues congratulate him for his courage. Friends say, "She was never good enough for you." But I'm suspicious that there's something markedly sexist at work here—a man leaving his wife is far more acceptable than a woman leaving her husband.

Ultimately, I must find peace with myself, not in or with David. This truth becomes clearer every day. I become too clingy— I need David to justify my presence in this place that's empty of history, roots, or purpose. The only purpose of my being here is to divorce myself from Paul so I can plan a future with David. But any future is at least six months away. I must build my own resources, find some strength of my own, to be better suited for that future. I know these things, but it's not easy. Maybe I'm too hard on myself. After all, it's my first day without children here, the fifth since the move—adjusting has to take time.

This apartment is so transient, a place to pass the time until we can begin a life. And yet it's the beginning of our life together. Where, before, there were discreet meetings in fine, distant places with total privacy, now there's constant and inescapable stress and more to come. This week David must tell his parents, his sister, and his children the new realities. There'll be more lawyer talk prohibiting our living together. Sherry calls us fools and idiots for living together—she says David will suffer great financial losses and I may lose custody of my children, if we persist. But we can't imagine living another way; our emotional needs are too great.

I'm urged by all to seek counseling and I realize I need it, but I'm enormously resistant (three times I've canceled appointments). The stress and the anguish are constant for both of us. The incredible things we must pass through to get to each other in the end. Can anything survive this? It's unimaginable I'd abandon David after what we've been through, but I do lose sight of the reasons. That hopefulness, that sense of opportunity and excitement we promised each other gets submerged in the exterior pressures—the ugliness and demands.

Never has life been like this for me, and yet, it's entirely of my choosing. Paul said, "The degree of your current dislocation is directly proportional to the degree you repressed dissatisfaction with your life these past two years."

Thursday, January 16

David has done it all—everything. He loves me with force, loyalty, and patience. His is a love of enormous consideration, tenderness, and deep, deep passion. He wants only to make me happy, and I thwart him by being unhappy, by continuing to be plagued by doubts. I need badly to talk to someone to clear my head.

When I light the bedroom candle for David and me, I look at a matchbox that says "Wintergreen"—and I think of my vacation there with Paul in September. I get a cup of coffee for David, and I stumble on the blue cup Paul brought me as a gift from a business trip. I miss the way Paul thinks and talks and challenges me. I miss the familiarity.

What I want is to love David forever, to make a life with him.

This is what I want. But I also want to leave Paul with a clear mind and heart. I now fear that all choices lead to unhappiness—and all David wants is for me to be happy. Paul and I may never be happy together, but we pose fewer problems for each other: the children cease to loom as a huge issue; we simply continue, to a large degree, to maintain the status quo. With David, everything is change, problematic, an issue to be resolved. The pressure on us is overwhelming. Yet there's a core to us—that's so pure and good and exciting and ego-stroking and satisfying that I could not consider abandoning it. When he looks at me, as he did over dinner last night, his eyes filled with all that spirit, I just want to take his hand, walk into our future, and forget the rest.

Things progress with the heavy dose of reality that everyone predicted. I find myself in lawyers' offices listening to discussions of Linda's alimony (I don't *want* to be part of that). I find myself jealous of the time he spends with his children (and ashamed of myself for feeling that). I find myself filled with unending guilt about Paul (I have danced off with David, barely glancing back at Paul's pain—and this is a wrencher). The money I take from David makes me exceedingly uncomfortable (it backs me into a corner). Maybe David and I need some unpressured time—maybe we'll never have that again.

Friday, January 17

Something must be said about the children's adjustment. Andrew cries hysterically every day he goes to his sitter's, Mary's. I begged, cried and pleaded on Andrew's behalf and bought a grudging month more. Max tells me he hates me and wants to live with his dad *all* the time—then he panics and rescinds it—"No, I want to be with you all the time." He tells Paul and then me the story of his imaginary friend, Giova, who dies. "You see," he says, "his mommy and daddy were getting divorced, but when he died they decided not to." Paul and I relate the story to one another with horror. There are days at school when Max's teacher reports he is crying easily and complaining of stomachaches—

it's clear he's having trouble swallowing food. He's tense, a child who holds it all in. We've not seen the tip of that iceberg.

All of this, every bit of this, tears me apart—causes me enormous guilt. My babies, my happy, well-adjusted little boys, growing up strong and healthy and loved and then—*wham!* the rug is pulled abruptly from beneath them and they struggle to find a way to land on their feet. Max keeps repeating before he goes to bed each night—almost a litany—"Mom, I still don't understand about this divorce business. You know I'm only five."

Monday, January 20

Good things have happened for me in these past days. I've been turned around. I'd written brief letters to my three closest women friends in Cleveland, Baltimore, and Chattanooga last week. They were the briefest of notes, spelling out the bare outline of my anguish, but clearly I was reaching out. This weekend, within hours of receiving my letter, each of these women called, talked on the phone for hours, and poured her enormous love and affection over me. These friends have roots in my childhood or early womanhood. All three remain good friends of Paul, but each took extra care to reach out to me and it was wonderful.

I have felt so abandoned and I do know the irony of saying this (me, who did the abandoning). I have felt so very alone and again feel the irony (me, who has found this compelling love). I have felt so overwhelmed with confusion and ambivalence about my future (me, who opted for the excitement of that future). But in three swift sweeps of the wand, all that was gone— the abandonment, the loneliness, the fear. Ronnie, Susan, and Emily—in their distinctive ways—picked me up and set me on my feet. Mostly, they let me talk. And each had the loyalty to be outraged at the treatment by my local friends.

Susan, divorced and a counselor, saw my plight in feminist terms and said: "Everyone fears a woman who does what she wants to do. Men fear the loss of power, women feel inadequate, and the notion threatens to upset the entire division of power.

In other words, men don't want to think their wives would and women don't want to think that they could. Also, people always seem to believe that they must make a choice, to decide who is wrong and who is right. The decision helps them defend against the anxiety that is stirred up in them—the possibility of choice becomes terrifying, so morality offers a safe answer that upholds the status quo. . . . A small town also needs gossip to unify and to stimulate it. This, too, will pass. You must rise above the storm and not get caught up in it, especially by allowing it to affect your decision-making processes. It all sounds awful and I feel for you deeply."

Ronnie, an artist married to an academic, confessed to a difficult midlife passage of her own and to seeing a psychiatrist since last summer. "Therapy is the best present you can give yourself," she said.

Emily, who has entertained Paul and me many times in Chattanooga, invited David and me to come for a visit and some necessary time away from here. I feel loved again.

It's important to describe what a friend my lawyer has become. Sherry is my age, Jewish, also married to a Catholic and from New York. After one consultation with a different lawyer, David hired Sherry to represent him as well. David has already filed for divorce. We meet publicly only in Sherry's office. "We've got to stop meeting like this," I jest. We sit in her office on the main street of town and the three of us chat about life—some charges on David's time, some on mine, some Sherry absorbs. Sherry genuinely cares about David and me; she always has her thumb on the pulse of our relationship. When Dave went alone to her office one day, she issued a long and thoughtful lecture on "Inette's compromised position in this town," on "Inette's sacrifice." She planned to have us over for dinner, but her husband, a friend of Paul's, vetoed that. Sherry and I understand one another, she likes David, and she's a fine lawyer. She gives her all.

Parenthetically, Paul absolutely refuses to see a lawyer. He insists he doesn't want a divorce and will not give me one. The no-fault divorce laws in this state specify "irreconcilable differences" as the grounds, and Paul says that we don't have "irreconcilable differences." "This is not a marriage that should end," he says. "We have our problems but all marriages do, and ours was damned good." So he resists.

The final contributor to my better frame of mind is Dr. Charles Berman, psychiatrist. A counselor friend of mine, Jack, took it upon himself to become an activist for my sanity. He called Dr. Berman, who practices two hours away in Asheville, offered to babysit for my children, and literally forced me to go. Still, when Dr. Berman was running late, I raged at him and was prepared to walk out his office door—so great was my resistance to therapy. I'm very, very glad that I did not. I talked for over two hours without letup, though he did respond and direct me. He ignored some things I thought were important, and he pointed to areas I've never considered. He asked me to describe myself, and because he is blind, I described myself physically. I found myself giving a very erotic description. He immediately turned the conversation to my father: "What," he asked, "was your relationship like with your father as a child?" Then he asked about my social and sexual life in adolescence. He's exactly what I need—a totally neutral listener, with absolutely no ax to grind, no point of view to defend, no motive other than the promotion of my good health. I respect and like him. He is a pro. He's a couple years younger than I and I call him by his first name. I feel a hundred times better than before my session with Charles Berman.

Friday, January 24
I've now had two long sessions with C. Berman, and my confidence is slowly being restored. I'm hustling work and loving it. After these long years with small children, neglecting my need to work, to haggle, to bully the world on my own energetic behalf—here I am again. I'm driven by the need to redeem my sense of self (I'm not solely Max and Andrew's mother or David's lover), and I realize it's a drive as old as these hills around me.

But I'm also driven by the very real need to make money. David pays for the apartment, Paul pays something toward the children's groceries, but I have bills—lawyer, psychiatrist, joint Visa card bills, and others—that are my sole responsibility. I'm searching for a way to meet them.

I will be teaching a creative writing and a journalism class at the community college next month. I've never taught before, and the idea of teaching what I've always done but never talked about is intriguing—fun to do at least once. I search for part-time work during this tough transition because I must devote a substantial chunk of time to the children. I put out writing feelers to old bosses and journalist chums, and that feels good, too. I'm working hard to sell the story I wrote last year, before the affair diverted my attention. I'm feeling my professional oats, and it's already obvious that being involved in my own work enhances my relationship with Dave. I'm no longer sitting here awaiting his arrival and dreading his sudden departure to a laboring woman.

Sunday, January 26

There's been a wonderful domesticity about these past weeks. Already I refer to the time preceding our cohabitation as "the affair." David loves being met at the door with a kiss—Linda never did that. But I always have—first with my father, then with my husband, now with David. David loves my constant chatter, my stream of consciousness talk that always drove Paul crazy. David loves my effusiveness (especially when I'm effusing over him)—Paul found it excessive. And David is inordinately proud of my hustling after work (his wife held a job only briefly, fifteen years ago).

After that first horrible week, this time together has been a breather—refreshing and delightful. I love having David's safari hat hanging on the poster of my bed; I love seeing his shoes next to the door, his teeth-rotting Pepsi in the fridge. This is the most consoling and healing kind of domesticity; it in no way threatens my self. I'm grateful for this time.

I'm even loving this place—it's small and manageable, unlike the huge farmhouse with its constant upkeep. Everything here is compact, my furniture looks great here, the place is bright—it's a perfect first home for us.

In the evenings, when the kids are in bed, Dave prepares tasteful and splendid dinners for me. He shoots a pheasant, cleans it, cooks it, sets a glorious candlelit table, and serves me his meal. The romantic David puts on his favorite Chopin tape, and as we eat, his eyes sparkle and he explains the music to me. I'm so taken with his competence, his range of ability, his sincerity, his love. He cleans up afterward.

On Sundays when he's not on call, he'll do a wonderful breakfast for the boys and me. He does his own laundry, irons his own shirts, sews his own tears (he is, after all, a surgeon). I think how much I've done for Paul over these years. I was the sole seamstress, food preparer, laundress, vacation planner, carpenter. Paul wasn't unwilling—simply unable, and no doubt I fed that dependence.

Have I written that Paul was never able to tell me, "I love you?" I have always had to ask, and that is not the same as being freely offered the words and feelings. But David is a whole other story—he lavishes his sincere, loving words without restraint. He tells me that I make *him* feel loved—for the first time in his life! We do that for each other.

Laughter—my God, we do laugh together. With Paul, I've been so serious. I've always been the straight man to Paul's wry and clever wit. My husband virtually defined me as humorless, and I bought it. But David finds me uproariously funny—flat-out funny. We do laugh together.

Sex is extraordinary. When I think it can't get better, it does. Every night, every morning without fail, and often without sleep. Very often, we just awaken to each other's touch from the dead of sleep and find ourselves groggy but ready to love. Now I function day after day with only a couple hours of interrupted sleep. It's as though David's remarkable energy is contagious.

The children: What a surprise and bonus they have been. I watch with great wonder as David falls in love with little Andrew, reveling in his babyness, the way no one has ever done. Andrew has always been a hugger, and now he snuggles against David and rushes to the door to greet him shouting, "Davey, Davey!" And Max who never tells anyone, "I love you," tells David that. Max wants so badly to love this man his mommy loves. Nothing touches me more than watching David play checkers with Max— cleverly setting up my son for his first win. Nothing moves me more than David reading bedtime stories to the boys in that flat Midwestern voice. There's a lot of genuine affection on both sides. But I feel a pang for Paul who incessantly hears enthusiastic tales of David from his sons. "If he ever does a thing to hurt those boys," Paul once said, "I'll kill him."

And it isn't altogether easy for David, either. He is kind to my boys, but he desperately misses his own two children (Debra, ten, and Steve, seven). When Max and Andrew climb into bed with us on Sunday morning, pushing and pummeling David play-fully, he gets a wistful and distant look and confesses to wrench-ing memories of Sunday mornings with his own sweet children. What is it that I can say to this? What can I offer him for his loss?

Monday, January 27
This is—would have been—my sixteenth wedding anniver-sary. I sent this note to Paul.

I can't help but be optimistic for each of us. There has been so much love we have given and taken, each in our own way over the years. But we have extracted a price, each of us from the other—a price that ultimately is too high in human spirit to pay. Is it that we have loved one another despite ourselves? Did I love you in spite of the person you are, and you me? I think so. How peculiar to be loved, but not liked—to be loved only at the expense of renunciation of the self we each knew we were.

So I'm optimistic for each of us. We are, you and I, lovable for the selves we are—we don't have to believe about ourselves that we're weak or inadequate or incompetent or stupid to be loved. Of this I am certain.

So realize I'm writing this letter for me. Because for some reason, in this process of separating ourselves from one another—on this day, January 27—I feel a need to express some thoughts to you and yes, in the midst of my happiest and fullest days, a certain sadness, too.

And Paul responded.

I suppose we did love each other despite ourselves. I knew from the beginning that loving you meant that I would be overwhelmed. Maybe that is why I always had such trouble saying it out loud to you. And there I was, shortly after you broke the news, saying for the first time, straight to your face, with no reservation, "I love you," precisely as you slipped out of my arms. There's a song by Marshall Crenshaw I've grown to appreciate lately called "Terrifying Love." That is how it looked from my point of view. I both feared and loved you. Perhaps the fear was more fundamental, but love did grow, despite everything else.

"She left me for another man"—the oldest story in the world. I'm lonely, I'm confused, I'm struggling, but there is no alternative. Yes, the shattering of our marriage has enabled me to see many possibilities for myself; yes, the shattering of my life has been somehow liberating. But that doesn't erase the pain.

When I see you, you look so fine. When I hear you I feel that uncomfortable fear. It is very difficult for me to be near you—my eyes tell me one thing, my mind another, and my heart a third.

Wednesday, January 29
I alerted Paul last week that I was coming back to the house today to pick up the freezer, Max's dresser, a small bookcase, and a rocking chair. I told him that I was borrowing a truck, and since he well knows that Wednesday afternoons are David's

time off, I assumed he realized David would help me move. I
expected Paul would be at work.

I arrived at the farm before David, who was picking up the
truck. Paul's pickup truck was still parked there and I was sick.
There was another truck that I recognized as Howard's, our re-
pairman. The water pipes had frozen and burst last night, flooding
the downstairs laundry room and ruining all sorts of family pictures and papers stacked there. The pipe burst in the worst possible place, and the bathroom tile upstairs had to be ripped out.
It was a mess. In my absence, the house has progressively de-
teriorated, but today it looked disastrous. Old habit dies hard,
and I attacked Paul. "Damn it, Paul, if you'd push up the ther-
mostat and burn some oil, this wouldn't happen." Paul and I
have fought with great predictability each winter about how to
heat the drafty old farmhouse. Paul wants to save fuel and cut
back the furnace—he thinks the woodstove is adequate, but I
do not. Paul was obviously feeling enormous guilt over the burst
pipes, but I could not resist the jab—it's in the nature of our
relationship.

Then I warned Paul that David was coming to help me move—
that he would probably want to leave for work. Paul was unequivocal—he would *not* leave. For some absurd reason, I moved
on to the issue of the typewriter. On some days it feels as though
the whole of our separation hinges on the issue of who owns the
electronic typewriter. Paul has it, I want it. I say my parents
gave it to me last Christmas; he says they gave it to both of us.
I say, "I need that typewriter for my work, and you are being
punitive. He says, "You'll never get this typewriter, *never.*" And
so it went today. At this point, Howard, trying his damnedest
to ignore us, left for town to buy some pipe.

This is what happened. For one half-hour, Paul beat me up.
He dragged me by my hair, hurled me against walls, threw me
into tables, yanked me to my feet, and slammed me across rooms.
All the while, he held a heavy, clublike flagpole inches over my
head and screamed that if I moved he'd kill me. I never doubted

that he would. I was terrified, terrorized, and sobbing hysterically. "Get out of here this minute," he'd order; but I was petrified to move with that club over my head. This scene began in the front hall and moved in fits and starts the forty-five or fifty feet to the kitchen. There, he grabbed a knife and held it next to my head. I was in acute pain—my head had hit the corner of the picnic table (now in the dining room), and I was aching and throbbing all over. The abuse and the beating seemed endless, and then there was the knife. I slowly crawled to the silverware drawer with every intention of grabbing a knife myself. At that point, Paul pulled me off the floor and shoved me out the door into the cold, wet January day. I left the yard, leaned against the car, and sobbed my heart out.

Finally, David arrived. I told him what happened and he could not digest it, could think of nothing to justify the physical abuse. "I can understand beating me up, but why *you?*" I answered, "Because he rightly sees me, not you, as the cause of his distress." David did the only thing he could do—he held me close to him and comforted me.

This was the first time Paul had seen David and me together. Paul walked out onto the porch with a tire iron in his hand, glared at David Muller, and said, "If you so much as put a finger on the doorknob of my house, I swear I will break your fucking hands. I will start with your hands and then move to your balls." David and Paul stood maybe ten feet apart, looking eye to eye— Paul was full of venom, David was silent, full of remorse and guilt.

After Paul had beat me and threatened my life, terrorized me in ways no one in my life has ever done, all I could think was, "He must not be allowed to get away with this—to think this was possible, an acceptable option." I had every intention of filing a warrant for his arrest. He would have been arrested in our small town, required to post bond and appear in court. But, hours later, when I sat in Sherry's office, exhausted and hurting from head to foot—my head covered with egg-size knots, my cheekbone swollen, my neck immobilized—I decided not to. Sherry allowed that it was my choice to make. She laid out all the legal options, and I said, "David, get me out of here."

It was neither love nor empathy that stopped me. I no longer feel either of those. It was just, "What the fuck, what's the point?" Instead, I told Sherry to file the divorce suit—enough of this gentle persuasion. The sheriff will serve Paul divorce papers tomorrow.

Thursday, February 6
The day after the beating, Paul wrote me this letter.

I want to write one last personal note to you before all of this moves into the legal arena. Of course, as I sit here at two in the afternoon, I know that this had already become a legal situation some time ago. I was just slow to realize it, to begin to participate in it. Thus, this cannot be as personal as I might wish. I did want to say that I am sorry for how I treated you yesterday— that is, I want to express my shock at my own behavior, primarily because it broke a cardinal rule between you and me.

I did not want to go to a lawyer because that meant that I wanted a divorce. I told my lawyer quite clearly that I do not want a divorce, and I explained that I feel that way because— after all the soul-searching I've done, after all the examination of our relationship, after all the pain I endured, after all the anger I've felt—I still believe that the problems between us are not insurmountable. This marriage can be saved. Therefore, the hardest thing for me ever to forgive will be the helpless sense that, as I said yesterday, you never gave me a chance. As your husband of sixteen years, I deserved better than that.

Nothing is ever linear. Amazingly, there continue to be quiet, decent moments with Paul. He'll pick up the kids or drop them off and be sweet, caring, and solicitous. He'll bring me tapes of music he's assembled that speak to his current emotions, and oddly, the music speaks to me in ways that he no longer can.

But the decent moments are quickly obliterated by violent ones. He arrives to exchange children and hurls boxes of my old letters, old professional and personal papers, at my back porch. As he strews my things, he screams obscenities, calling me a whore and worse for all my neighbors to hear. We have become a soap opera. It all feels so tacky, so low-class, so sleazy. And it is *us*— decent, respectable, good, loving, intelligent, thoughtful people—trapped in some incredible scenario of ugliness.

Inside the strewn boxes I find nineteen years of photographs of Paul and me—each with Paul carefully snipped out. It is so sad. There we are sipping from each other's wine glass, twenty years old, in Florence, Italy—and Paul is gone. He's gone, too, from family Christmas pictures, from wedding pictures, from photos with the children. It is so very sad. The *Just Married* sign that my brothers attached to our honeymoon car, which hung for ten years sentimentally over our bed, was shredded and stuffed into one of the boxes. In another, there was my Bat Mitzvah picture—thirteen-year-old Inette preening in white lace—now pasted over with pornographic photos of women with spread legs, now captioned, *Whore Princess.*

Monday, February 10

David and his family are, of course, an ongoing issue, but in a much subtler way than the very overt push and pull of Paul and me. Often David storms around in anger at Linda, "Shit, she *never* loved me at all, she never even *liked* me. She just likes the idea of my being the husband and father." He tells a story of falling off his horse last year and badly injuring his back. He says that he crawled on his belly some distance to the house, to Linda "and she wouldn't even touch me, wouldn't put her hand on me."

Because David earns a great deal of money, their divorce proceedings are far more complicated that Paul's and mine. No, let me change that—mine are more emotionally complicated, his are more fiscally complicated. Linda, like many abandoned women, directs her anger at their pocketbook, where it seems to enrage

David effectively. "She never contributed a thing to this marriage," he rages. "I cooked, I furnished the house, I sewed, I entertained."

But the continuing crux of their divorce is the children. Linda mercilessly uses them in her search for revenge. They have signed a temporary separation agreement spelling out financial and visitation issues. Linda was adamant that the agreement prohibit the children from ever seeing their father in my presence. I don't blame her one bit, but of course it hurts and embarrasses me. Far more important, it makes it mighty difficult for Dave to be more than a restaurant/movie/shopping mall dad. Linda has more than once reneged on David's visiting nights. "The children have other plans," she'll say, or "I don't feel well, I don't want to see you." David has legal recourse, but he is too filled with guilt to exercise it. In all matters concerning their children, he by habit defers to Linda. That is the nature of their relationship. He silently fumes and is effectively pained to be deprived of his children, but he permits Linda full control over when he sees them. It's the one area of their marriage where Linda exercises control and she uses it cleverly and effectively. My hat is off to her. But Paul and I have been exceedingly cautious not to use our children as tools of revenge, and I'm proud of that fact.

Saturday, February 15

It's a snowy, lovely morning in this small town. The children are with Paul, David is at work, and this gives me some much-needed time for myself. The intensity of this new relationship, the wanting to seize all moments with David, has prevented me from carving out these nice quiet moments for myself. This day feels good. This week has been my best yet—partly because Paul and I are not communicating at all, just exchanging necessary information about the children. There can be coldness, but no open hostilities, and that's an enormous relief to me. I hate the intense ups and downs. Now it boils down to a monthly schedule of child exchange.

I'm tempted to write here a compendium of all that David and

I have become together. There's so much comfort, so much growing familiarity, and yet that has in no way undermined the romance. I'm far less threatened by time—time to discover each other before divorces and remarriage. Earlier, that time seemed threatening, but now it's sort of exciting. I do love the discovering. There remains a lot for David and me to know. There remain tests and trials to run, but I look forward to them.

I do miss seeing David in a social context. We're almost always alone. We plan dinner parties, but they always get bogged down on the guest list. My friends? Who is still talking to me? His friends? Will they feel awkward coming here? We love planning the menus, that's infinitely easier—he does the fish, I do the key lime pie. One night, at the insistence of his two colleagues, we went to a restaurant with these men and their wives. There was, of course, in the invitation implicit approval of David's decision—that and great curiosity about me. I actually had fun, but I know that David felt very awkward replaying a social scene he'd often played with Linda.

Of course, we'll have to leave this town to make a real life for ourselves. We'll have to find new places and neutral faces. We'll have to find friends that are "ours." We will need a fresh start, and to that end, David continues his search for an equally lucrative practice somewhere else. We try hard to balance his search for a medical practice with my search for a renewed career. We try to balance his need of country with my need of city. We often get balled up in our conflicting needs. None of this is easy.

Monday, February 17

With continuing therapy—two-hour sessions with Charles Berman every Friday—I'm coming out of this stronger. My lawyer disapproves of David's and my living together for legal reasons, but my psychiatrist is opposed for altogether other reasons. "It is too soon," he says. He fears my financial dependence on David—that money will be the tie that binds. He fears I too willingly sacrifice my needs to David's. David is needlessly threatened by my therapy; he sees C. Berman as an instrument of sabotage.

He is sure that Dr. Berman will convince me to give him up. After each two-hour session, there is a two-hour rehash of the session with David. (And it's funny that Paul sees the sessions as a reason for hope.) Neither man is on target. The therapy is the one thing I do entirely for me.

Still it's important to realize that, side-by-side with the increased peacefulness in my life, I have developed a genuine horror of what I've done to Paul. What I've done is unthinkable, unimaginable, cruel. I'm consumed with guilt. It amazes me that Paul survives at all—the rest of his antics aren't so surprising. Am I without shame? Is shame quite beside the point? My lawyer, Sherry, says of these feelings, "Ahh, Inette—he has finally gotten to you. He has finally succeeded in getting to you." And that is true. I'm no more willing to return to him, but I'm stricken daily by what I do to him. Can the love of another man justify this? And yet, that's the only justification I have—nothing else holds water.

But I also know how intense was my despair these past two years: how dead I was, how dead Paul was, how inadequate was my parenting. All real life was dormant. We plodded on the path we'd carved for ourselves many years before. It was a path that worked well for us for years, but ultimately failed to work at all. It became my trap. So all that's happening to me now *had* to happen. And perhaps all this had to happen for Paul, too. I'm not convinced that it had to happen *like this* for Paul, yet maybe there was no avoiding the pain.

I feel that I'm doing the right thing for me—ultimately, the only thing I could do for me—and, truth be told, in the only way *I* could do it. My behavior since October is probably completely consistent with my style of doing things (impatient, impulsive, given to action), if not consistent with my character (faithful, loyal, and monogamous). So if not in this affair with David, then I'd probably indulge in some other equally forceful mode of behavior. That makes David—whatever else he is—at least the instrument by which I free myself from my marriage. This, right now, is a revelation.

But what about Paul? Is all this essential for him? Is this the only way change could happen for him—through me—the only way it *has* happened for him in nineteen years? I don't yet have the answers and I'm plagued with guilt.

Friday, February 21

Today Charles Berman felt threatening. He looks at times too much like an advocate for my marriage. On a good day, with a bit of distance, I can see that he wants only for me to examine the real issues of my marriage before I plunge into another. "I worry about you and David five years down the road," he says. He repeatedly tells me to slow down. But today I was plenty pissed at Berman, and I told him in no uncertain terms to "quit cramming Paul down my throat."

Thursday, February 27

Perhaps Linda competes with another woman for her husband. But I compete with her husband's work. I've always been intensely jealous of the time David gives his job. For thirteen solid days now, David has been on call, covering for his partner on vacation in Florida. That means, for thirteen interminable days, our life has been at the mercy of the damn beeper or the telephone. I'm unused to this—Paul always devoted a lot of time to the family—his work clearly came second. David, however, can be eating dinner, showering, jogging, or making love—and when the phone rings, he'll ask "How many centimeters?" and then he'll be gone. My assumption has been that he loves his work, loves to make money, and prefers both to an active personal life—so I've occasionally felt slighted. But last night, his partner returned and David was freed from his beeper. He came dancing into the apartment full of smiles, full of himself, full of plans for us. And a bell went off in my head—he, too, is oppressed by work, by constantly being on call. Here he was, visibly emerging from an enormous weight; the burden was lifted. So I learned a lesson about David today. I learned that though he certainly loves his work and needs it, he is beaten by it, too.

This man's life is not his own. He does surgery from 7:30 A.M. to noon on Monday, Wednesday, and Friday. He has office hours all day Tuesday and Thursday, plus Monday and Friday afternoons and Saturday morning. He is on call to deliver babies during all office hours, on Tuesday and Thursday nights, and on alternate weekends. He can count only on Wednesday afternoons and alternate weekends off—when he *still* has to check his hospital patients, do charts and "presurgical rounds." He makes a lot of money because he works a lot of hours. Apart from these incomprehensible hours, there are the unbelievably stressful demands of his job: a young mother with advanced uterine cancer; emergency surgery (a car wreck involving a pregnant woman, in which the baby died); a life-saving caesarean section; a deformed baby. David is a very, very fine surgeon and an exceptionally adept obstetrician. This isn't just my personal reading, it's the professional consensus. He's conscientious, he's kind, he's competent, and he's working all the time.

So I begin to understand what the country, the out-of-doors is for this man. The trout streams and the national forests are more than a hobby—they're the necessary antidote to the constant pressure of his work. These Appalachian mountains—their solitude, their soothing lack of demands, their absolute unyielding physical nature are the yin to David's medical yang. This I begin to understand. And though I can share only the stories from his work and not the work itself, I *can* share the country. I can and do walk with David through the forests with shotgun in hand—climbing the steep hills, tripping over vines, listening for birds, relishing the leisure. I can stand next to a still trout stream with flyrod in hand and concentrate on his casting instructions, laughing at his impatience with my ignorance. I can share these quiet moments. Being in the woods and mountains with this man I love is the very best of times for me. David has doubts that my interest in the outdoors is genuine; he believes I do these things to please him. But he is very wrong. Trap shooting on a doctor friend's abandoned hilltop farm is fantastically invigorating. It's a whole other world opening to me—a world too long denied this suburban girl. I love it for itself, and I love it because I share it with David.

Monday, March 3

I have a lot of trouble writing about this past weekend. It was bad, maybe the worst yet. It set off waves that still pound these shores. Paul called me Saturday night and he was very drunk. For almost two hours he abused me, pulled my emotional strings, and I listened. Then he called back and went after David for an hour—he listened, too. "Why," Charles Berman asked me later, "didn't you say, 'I can't talk to you when you're drunk and abusive,' and then hang up?" But that was never an option—listening was the least I could do for the man I've treated so badly.

My friend Frances called from New York today and had her own explanation for why I listened to Paul. "I know you, Inette. You just don't want to give up control of Paul." I don't know, I don't know. Paul moves closer and closer to signing the separation agreement—which is tantamount to agreeing to a no-fault divorce—and I'm both afraid and glad. I'll never stop caring for Paul, feeling so much for him—or maybe I will, but it will take a long long time. Still, I do trust my instincts, which seem to be moving my life away from his (it feels self-protective, it feels like a search for some other thing to fill some other need).

There were many conflicting emotions this weekend. After the calls, I couldn't get Paul out of my mind, and I told David so. I lay awake all night wanting to call Paul, needing to talk to Charles Berman—not knowing what I would say to either one. David was very undermined by this "pull of Paul." He withdrew and counterattacked, "You'll never be able to live with my work." We reached an impasse. It felt like the end, and I was petrified. I had vague thoughts of suicide—vague, generalized hopelessness and loneliness. I could *not* go on without David. We both cried and we clung to one another and we're now slowly piecing ourselves together. But it's all very tentative and uncertain.

Yes, the weekend was bad, and I communicated the nature of that badness to Charles Berman by phone. I spoke of the black void that is my life without Dave—the all-encompassing blackness. I spoke of my existential terror of being alone. And Dr. Berman said quietly, "Inette, you might want to think about hospitalization—you might need to get away from David for a few days." Yet, as much as I fear that black emptiness, greater still is my fear of a mental hospital—a psychiatric hospital where I expect they'd fill me with drugs and take control of aspects of my life that that I'm unwilling to relinquish. "No, not that," I told Charles. "Okay," he said, "but you might want to keep it in mind."

Tuesday, March 4

I just sent still another solitary red rose to David's office. The single red rose, anonymously delivered by the florist to David at work—always after a particularly difficult day—has become my material offering to our relationship. I started in early January before our planned trip to Asheville, when David was very frightened of what we were about to do. When we met, I handed him the red rose, and he said, "No one has ever given me a flower." Over these months, when Linda is depriving David of his children, when he's confused and hurting, I send one lone rose to his office and he is soothed.

Monday, March 10

David and I spent the weekend at the lovely and elegant Ritz-Carlton Hotel in Washington, DC. It's the very definition of a small hotel: very personal service, peach tulips in the lobby, very low key. Every woman in the lobby had a fur. It was my first awareness of the difference that money can make—of the seductiveness of a man spending money to please you, of a man pampering you as though money were no object. I see what David means when he says that he wishes to take care of me. Still, I carry a very heavy suspicion of being "cared for" financially. David spent Saturday buying clothes for himself, and he wanted to buy an outfit for me. I gave him the hardest time before agreeing. I just don't feel comforable being bought presents by a man I'm not married to. Is this absurd? I did get a dress and modeled it for him (if he pays for it, he has some say about how it looks, right?). I wanted the red belt, he wanted the white— so I bought the white and felt sort of bought myself. David chooses all his wife's clothing.

Then, when I was shopping with David at Britches, he asked for my opinion of a sweater. "I like the sweater," I said, "but not the color." Abruptly, in front of the salesman he responded, "I like it, I'll take it." He totally rudely dismissed my opinion— the opinion *he* had solicited. I felt like shit. I'm not at all sure what was at work here. This is the first and only time he's ever been brusque or demeaning to me.

But apart from these shopping episodes, David and I had a glorious weekend. I used to live in Washington, and I loved showing David around. We saw the new Woody Allen movie, *Hannah and Her Sisters,* which Dave loved for its ethnicity (read *Jewishness*), and I found that endearing. He insisted we see my first Japanese movie, *Ran,* by the director Kurosawa. He warned me that Linda fell asleep during this fellow's movies and hated them, and from his description (epic, huge battle scenes) I was convinced that for the first time I would be lumped with Linda— that I, too, would hate his movies. Well, lo and behold, *Ran* was fantastic, visually extraordinary—a simple visual composition, with great acting, a compelling story—a grand, old, epic movie done artistically. I'm a convert. Saturday night we went to the Kennedy Center for the National Symphony, again David's turf, but again I like the challenge of his interests.

David, I've detected, is a real patsy for the ornate, for frill. I'm not sure he can distinguish between good design and opulence. He always goes for genuine leather, highly finished wood, executive office building goo. But then I continually underestimate David. I expect the years will cure me of that. David is the consummate traditionalist: he loves the inside of the National Gallery (so do I), but he is silent when I rave about the beauty of the new East Wing. He loves American realist art—the Hudson River school, and such—stuff I've always sneered at. But it's funny, lying in bed later, talking about the American art we'd seen that day, he was his most wonderfully eloquent and descriptive. God, he *can* describe things of nature—it's a gift. I can look at that painting and sneer, or stand in the woods and not see; but when David paints his visual picture, it's sharply in focus, crystal clear. Is that the city girl's dilemma? He tells stories of kayaking down the Mississippi River as a teenager; he describes the factories on the one side and the swamps, ducks, little inlets on the other. It comes alive for me. David calls himself an anomaly. That seems a bit much to me. He *is* different, complex, and a fascinating combination of people, but an *anomaly* is a bit much.

This weekend, too, was one of the few times we've been out with another couple socially. My old journalist friend Carol and her husband Omar joined us for dinner Saturday night after the orchestra. I worried that David would be uncomfortable with my old friends. He said that he was not, but he was quiet and withdrawn. They are, of course, kind of flashy and glib and David is neither. David insisted afterward that he loved being with my friends, "Watching the sparks fly between you and Carol." I do wonder what Carol and Omar thought of David. I *am* curious.

David, away from work, is a whole other person. He becomes again the person I've been meeting in discreet and distant places all autumn. Sex between us becomes ever more exhilarating. I've read that women in their late thirties peak sexually, just as men of that age have begun a decline—so here is where they meet most perfectly. Men take longer to climax, allowing women lots of time for multiple and then more multiple orgasms. That's how it is for David and me—his incredible energy and staying power, my inexhaustible passion and need. In bed he says, "You spoil me." "For what?" I ask. He speaks his fantasy, "You are my slave girl," and he laughs and laughs at the idea.

Tuesday, March 18

For the first time since we've lived together, Dave and I were apart for two days and nights. He took his children to Washington this weekend. Anticipating the time apart, I dreaded it. It turned out to be a lovely time for me. Friday and Saturday nights were mine without intrusion (after Andrew and Max were asleep). There was no waiting for David to come and go, no having to fit my life around his. The first night I wrote letters, the second night I worked at my writing. On Sunday, I took the kids out to breakfast at Shoney's and then swimming at the local indoor pool. In sum, I was surprised to find myself loving the time to myself. Charles Berman will be delighted to hear me say this on Friday.

David's trip, however, irritated the hell out of me for one concrete reason. It was an exact duplication of our trip last weekend. He took the kids to Washington, drove in the Jag, stayed at the Ritz Carlton, ate breakfast where we had on Capitol Hill, strolled the National Gallery. I suggested all sorts of alternatives: alternative cities, alternative hotels, alternative sites. I made it clear that his duplicating the trip for his children out of guilt detracted from the pleasure of my own trip. Still, he persisted.

He did come back hours earlier than expected because he missed me. He conceded that it wasn't nearly as pleasurable the second time with children (Well, I would *expect* not.) And he brought me back a magnificent brass cappuccino machine, like the one we'd admired three and a half months ago in Boston. He took me to dinner Sunday night when he returned and talked. He said that he had been obsessed with guilt over Linda and the children ever since our trip to Washington. But, he said, this weekend resolved some issues for him: "I know I'll always have a relationship with my children." At dinner he seemed so appreciative of me.

Thursday, March 20

For the past two and a half weeks, Paul has been in California visiting his family, and the children have been my sole responsibility. It's been exhausting. Until I moved out of the farm last January, I was a woman who had never given her children a bath—that was always Paul's job. Paul also fed them breakfast, put them to bed at night, and cared for them completely on weekends. He's always been an active and involved father, and I've always been accustomed to joint parenting. These two and a half weeks with absolutely no relief from Paul have been demanding. I drove the children to their school and sitter near the farm and killed an hour of my writing time at each end of every day. Still, I'd gotten used to the boys' defining my time or lack of time these weeks—and now Paul is back and they are gone; I feel their absence acutely.

Paul arrived at two o'clock to pick up the boys and didn't leave until four. We both seemed eager to share his California trip, to treat one another kindly. He was full of family stories— this family we've shared for sixteen years—and I was delighted to hear them. What was his sister up to? Had our niece dropped out of college? Was his brother still playing the drums? Had his parents' home been sold? "Your two weeks away from the boys has been hard on them," I said. "This is the longest you and I have been apart," he answered. We spoke for two straight hours, exchanging family news and warm feelings. At one point, I reached out and touched his arm. When he left, we hugged each other—a nice, nonthreatening, endearing hug. Since he's left, I lie here thinking about him and his sweet face and—yes, as insane as it seems—I even think we can still make a life together. Life with Paul always seems so much easier than that which must be worked out with David. Oddly, I feel this despite the fact that David and I are full of plans for a trip to New Hampshire to check out a medical practice—full of excitement and, of course, full of fear. Am I crazy?

Saturday, April 5

I'm having trouble breathing. Paul delivered the children, brought a few artifacts from our life together (my college diploma, my mother's journalism book, and the kids' bank books), and as he backed the truck out, he quietly said, "Oh, by the way, when we see each other next, we'll be divorced. I ask one thing—that you don't drag it on, that you let me get on with my life."

I don't know what I feel. Divorce seemed down the road— I'd come to depend on Paul's resistance. "He's your safety net," David accused me last night. I'm feeling numb—neither happy nor sad—just numb. I called David and told him what had happened. He wasn't surprised. I called Charles Berman and he was unavailable. I just want to keep calling, to talk to someone— otherwise, there's just the mirror with my face in it, alone. Divorced.

Last night—only last night—David talked about the ever-present Paul in my life. "No wonder *you* don't feel ghosts and demons," he said. "You *still have* Paul in your life." I had asked David how he felt about Paul moving to nearby Boston "to be near the boys"—if we moved to New Hampshire. And he spat at me, "I'd feel nauseated." David deserves more than I give. I hang on to Paul and think that David doesn't notice. Last night, at the Chinese restaurant, he made it very clear that he's fully aware of my hedging.

In fact, the more I know David, the better I like him and the more I trust our relationship. This weekend in New Hampshire was very reassuring. But lately I've come to feel that time is our ally. Now, with Paul insisting on the divorce—does that put little-needed pressure on David and me or does that just free me to get on with the life I've chosen? I don't know. David is good to me and for me, but ours will never be an easy relationship. Of course, there is no such thing as an easy one. Paul may have been the easiest I'll ever know.

Monday, April 7

David moved out one hour ago—lock, stock, and barrel. Toothbrush, desk, books, cassettes, rowing machine, and safari hat are gone. He's moved back to his friend John's. I'm uncertain that I can describe how this came about. I am heartsick. In a half an hour, he'll return to say good-bye to my sons. I wonder how I'll get through the night, how I'll get through the days— what life will be like without the calls from the hospital for David, without physician recruiters incessantly phoning with places for us to move? I wonder what it will feel like to sleep alone, to eat dinner alone, to be unloved. His closet in our room is empty. My chest is full. I am very, *very* scared.

This all began Saturday. First came Paul's announcement that he had signed the separation papers, then my panic, which I communicated to David. Then, Saturday night, David went to his house to see his children, who'd returned from a ten-day Easter vacation to David and Linda's Midwestern home town with their mother. David came back from that visit filled with shared family stories—and feelings exactly like mine when Paul returned from California. I knew that he felt ambivalence. There were German cookies baked by a favorite aunt and sent back especially for Davey. There were people and places that were points of reference only to the Mullers. There were two lives enmeshed for sixteen years. It was the first time David had allowed these supressed feelings to surface. "It was the first time in months her face wasn't contorted in hostility and sneers," he said of Linda. So he sat in the warmth of the house he'd always loved, with their children playing at his feet, and he was torn with confusion.

As I write this now, at 8:30 P.M., David sits behind me reading a bedtime book about dinosaurs to Max. He's reading in that flat Midwestern voice that's always so strangely entertaining to me, and it reminds me of the first days here in this apartment— the first time David read to the boys—and I remember melting into a puddle of gratitude for this man's sweetness to my sons. Now he just may be reading to them for the last time. He came over to say good-bye and, typically, brought the boys a whipped-cream-filled cake. Also typically, he and Max are having trouble finding the words to describe their feelings.

Max raced in this evening, immediately noticed that David's desk was gone, and laughingly asked where it was. I said, "David took it away," but Max was off and running trying to find where it had been moved. Finally I managed, "David isn't going to live here anymore." And Max burst into tears. "Why, why? I *want* him to live with us. Will he come back? Will he stay one more night?" But when David arrived, there was none of that. When Dave gave Max the cake, my son said: "You don't have to buy us things for us to love you." And David said, "Inette, you have very fine boys, your mother would be proud."

So how have we gotten here, to this place of such extreme sadness that if I turn around and look at David and the boys over there on the sofa, I'll begin to cry and not be able to stop?

Yesterday was a beautiful spring day, but I was again stuck home with sick kids. David went over to his house to fly kites and sail toy boats with Debra and Steven, the potential step-children I may now never really know. When he returned last night, I was in the shittiest of moods—trapped with sick children and bored. But, more than that, I was feeling distinctly unattended by David.

I forced the discussion and it went on throughout the night. I'm not even sure what all was said: David's confusion, David's ambivalence, David's need to be alone, David's fears for our future, David's terror of the compromises he's unaccustomed to making. Then, for the first time, he said that he needed "space." That awful, deadly word—*space*. He didn't even feel the weight of it, but God, I did immediately. And I said, with great effort, "Then you must move out."

I am shocked at the speed with which he borrowed that damn truck and packed up his things. He asked that I not be here when he was loading the truck, and for hours, I complied. But as the afternoon wore on, I panicked and knew I had to get back to the apartment before he left. I sped across the county roads and found the truck parked out back, completely full. David stood upstairs, leaning against the wall, clutching his toiletry case. He was absolutely colorless—his face completely drained. I hugged him, held him, and said simply, "David, don't do this." He moaned—there is no other word for it—he moaned, "Oh, Inette, this is much harder than leaving my house ever was."

Tuesday, April 8, Midnight

Yesterday David moved out of our home. Tonight, only this moment, we have ended our six-month-old affair. I sent still another red rose to his office this morning; he jogged over here at five o'clock and wound up staying until now. I just drove him back to the clinic and said "Good-bye."

We talked only the truth tonight, as best we could individually understand what the truth is. We cried honest tears and we just made the best love I've ever made in my life. David's eyes were open the entire time, "Because I don't want to miss a thing." Like when Pat Boone touched my arm when I was twelve and it remained unwashed for weeks, I expect my sheets will remain unchanged for a long time.

We talked tonight and we cried. But we affirmed our love, affirmed our friendship, affirmed our attraction to each other; and we seem to have decided that we must be apart—must return to our marriages. At this moment and ever since I climbed out of bed with David, I'm as happy as I've ever been. I'm totally satiated. If we can really end this affair on such a high and worthy night—great beginnings and great endings—we'll have done it up right.

I feel a genuine need to write a bit here about why David and I have ended this affair. I feel as though these sequential thoughts have omitted a great deal. The fact is, I'm not absolutely certain why this affair has ended now. Our attraction and energies are still at a peak. There has been *no* discernible diminishment of feeling on either part. So you must understand that ending this affair at a high point is and will be extremely painful—maybe even impossible, I don't know. But it appeals to my sense of completion. It's a classy way to end this affair.

For my part, there has always been an enormous well of unresolved feeling for Paul. This, Charles Berman has consistently seen and insisted it be dealt with. This, David has known and spoken of frequently. This, I have acknowledged to myself but have always denied to David. On David's part there has been enormous repression of feeling. He makes me look like a piker in the repression department—no mean feat. Increasingly, in recent weeks, the feelings he has buried have been breaking through. The children have always been the overwhelming symbol of his loss and of his failure. When the children were away for Easter, David ate his gut out with longing and called them daily. He tried to imagine living in New Hampshire with his children here in North Carolina, and he could not do it.

So perhaps David and I did not love each other enough—perhaps. Or perhaps our love is essential, the best of all relationships—but for the entanglement of our former emotional lives, still unresolved. I stand here rather proud of all I've done in this affair, I haven't a single regret. I loved David well and I still do. I wish that I had been able to make a life with him. I *still* do. But I'm accepting that that will not happen, that we are too laden with our former lives. I've never been happier than I've been with David. I've never given nor taken better love, and I can't renounce that love or those wishes. But I have to begin a life without them.

Later

After writing these words, I called Paul. Still full of myself, still oddly joyous, I told him what just happened. "No one is saying that you and David didn't have a wonderful relationship and couldn't have made a great life together," said Paul. "What I'm saying is that you never freed yourself from me, from your love of me."

And then he said, "Inette, I have loved you, I do love you. We could still be great together after all this, but you have to see *me*, not someone you want to mold, not some reflection of yourself—you have to see me warts and all." And then he waited— there was a long pause—and I knew I was supposed to say, "I love you Paul," but I did not. For some reason, I could not.

Part IV
DISENGAGING

Wednesday, April 9

Dearest Inette,
Please *know* that you are loved, cherished, admired and respected. Know also that you will always, always, always be remembered.

> Love,
> Dave

This note arrived attached to one dozen red roses and my joy vainished, my composure crumpled. What gesture and what words could have been more final?

Thursday, April 10
Paul mailed me a copy of this ten-page letter he sent to Charles Berman. It reads:

Dear Charles Berman:
So here's my position—divorce or reconciliation; it is that

straightforward. She panicked at the edge (another characteristic move) and that has opened a slight space for renewed conversation. I will not talk to her if she refuses to listen. I am talking to her with a heart filled with love, even when I called her a whore, when I drunkenly lashed out at her breathtaking selfishness—these words all came from a loving heart. But I am not going to waste that love any longer. I am not going to forfeit the personal gains I have made in living through what has been the greatest trauma of my life. I have not been able to kill the love I feel inside myself for Inette, but in this situation, as Tina Turner sings, "What's Love Got to Do with It?" What is important here is my basic sense of self, of self-worth, the preservation of those very good qualities I have allowed myself to recognize inside my person.

I raised two not-unrelated objectives. One, that Inette look at me directly and hopefully find that she likes what she sees; and two, that Inette look at herself directly and again likes what she sees. I guess it is pretty obvious that I figure one flows from the other—a person who likes herself is going to be able to love me a whole lot better. I don't expect any magical "quick fix" in Inette's self-perception—just the opposite, because she is such a tough bird or at least defines herself that way. I'm prepared to slug it out in the pits. I am not prepared to give up the fight as I have done so many times before. I even realize, I think, that slugging it out in the pits may not save the marriage. Maybe I've suffered more damage than I know. But the fact is that I insisted Inette move out of the house last January specifically because I believed she needed some time to examine herself and her behavior.

I know that one of the major tragedies of this affair is that there is no person better for Inette in the world during this time of crisis than me. I have become a better person as a result of this episode. I will be a better husband to her and, God help me, I'm willing to offer that new, improved version of myself to her if she will do likewise.

So, would it be appropriate for both Inette and I to talk to you?

My best wishes,
Paul Lucca

Friday, April 11

I'm staying with Carol and Omar in Washington for four days. I arrived yesterday. I'm sitting right now among the Braques and Cezannes in the Phillips Collection, writing and looking out of the window at the new spring leaves, the dogwood blossoms, and the Ritz-Carlton Hotel. Of course, I'm thinking of David. I have been making plans to move to Washington, plans to start up a magazine with Carol, but I do none of these things with more than half a heart. Nothing seems pressing, important, or compelling without David.

Saturday, April 12

I don't know what it is I want. I do know that if Dave stood before me, miraculously free of his "demons," of his need for space, of his "I'm confused, I don't know what I want" feelings— free of all the painful emotions he vented on me over a forty-eight-hour period—I would go to him. But short of that, I cannot. Because I know that I would choose David, if he were miraculously free of his doubts and wanted me enough, I can't go into therapy with Paul. That would be unkind, unfair, and wrong.

I have talked to a woman here about a $1,000-a-month, tiny apartment near Carol. My God—money? Schools?—it's all quite frightening. I think I'm in for some very rough and lonely times. And all I ever wanted was to be married, to love and be loved— and, very possibly, I will be alone with two small children and very little money in a city. Naturally the prospect scares me, but I can only take this load one day at a time.

How *will* I be able to handle the children, to cope with their competing needs for my dwindling resources? I sit here on the most spectacular of Washington spring days and watch the Potomac River and the kids from the International School picnic, swing, and play soccer; and I think that maybe I could do this alone, without Max and Andrew, but I won't have that luxury. I *cannot* do that to them.

I watch Carol and Omar fighting, going through a difficult time. But it's a very married, committed, difficult time, and it has its appeal. It's the appeal of being part of a couple that has enough invested to hate each other at times.

I've taken my good times and I will pay a price. I've done exactly as I pleased—selfishly, Paul would say—and now it's my turn to pay the piper. Funny how that is. This really is a time of my life not even remotely like any other. So I talk about starting a magazine and it really is pointless without a love in my life, without someone to tell my stories to, who will tell me his. My career has always been what a good love gave me the courage to engage in—never a replacement for loving and being loved. What have I wrought?

Sunday, April 13

I've just returned to my apartment from Washington. As I barreled down the interstate from DC to Watertown, I became increasingly frantic. Now I'm wound tighter than a spring—trying to unpack, trying to reread these last days of the journal. My heart is racing like mad, my face is heated and flushed. I am—in one word—*panicked*. This is terror. Ths is undiluted fear. What do I do? I need Dave like a drug, my body is in withdrawal. But I *can't* call him or write him—I'd wind up degrading myself, crawling for bits and pieces of what once was. God, it may well be impossible to be here in this apartment.

I am so completely alone! Call Paul? No, that's immoral. Call my mother? No, I can't handle that. *Where is David?* Hunting, fishing, with the kids? I want to search for his Jeep. Call Charles Berman? Shit, he's not on call today. So what the fuck do I do? I may well be a lost soul. On the drive back, I kept thinking (hoping) I might fall asleep behind the wheel of that car and all of this shit would be over. Am I suicidal? The phone just rang—shit, it was a physician recruiter for Dave. Shit! I am alone—I am *afraid!*

Monday, April 14

Blissfully, there are still no children. I'll pick them up this afternoon and have them for the long haul. I'm thinking of going to Baltimore on Saturday to visit my family for a week. Where is David? Is he at his friend's house? Is he in Montana visiting his sister and climbing the Rockies, as he said he might? But, of course, these days I never know where he is, who he is with, or what he does. "The hardest part," Paul said to me after I moved out, "is not knowing what's going on in your life."

I want to write David, to reach out in some way. Omar advised me, "As a man, I suggest you give him the space he needs." My mother said, "You must not pursue him." So it comes to this. I'm single again, playing male/female games.

I called my parents last night. I'd forgotten how the main support I can expect from my mother is her constant presence. She *is* stalwart, but she is not affectionate (like her daughter?), and despite her best efforts, she can be counted on to say the least compassionate thing. My father was quiet. But the call prompted my first tears since David left, and crying released that godawful panic I've felt.

It's evening now. What a day this has been! Paul and I were engaging in a necessary phone conversation about financial things—in the midst of all this we've been audited by the IRS. At the finish of business, I said to Paul, "I assume that you've told no one about David and me." He responded, "It's on the streets, Inette—David moved back in with Linda on Friday." My God, I was devastated. The corpse wasn't even cold. Everyone in this town knew *but* me—and then to hear it from Paul. I went absolutely crazy. I called Berman—not in. I called my mother—not in. I called my friend Jack—not in. Then, out of the blue, my friend Claire called—she'd heard and wanted to commiserate with the abandoned woman. (How else can it be perceived here?)

I cried, I called David names, she listened, I hung up. Jack called, bless his heart. "This is not your problem, Inette. You know how to live, you are alive. This is David's problem. Why would a man choose to go back to a cold and distant marriage? What's wrong with *him?*" Bless his heart, Jack helped a bit. Then Charles Berman returned my call. "David doesn't know what he wants now, this marriage will not last—but I don't want to give you hope." Of course, he has.

After this series of calls, I managed to pick up my children and to do a good job of mothering tonight. I'm proud of that— it wasn't easy. Max asked if David was going to Baltimore with us for Passover next week (this had been the planned introduction to my family). I said, "No, David has moved back with Linda and Debra and Steven." Max cried and cried. Then he got very angry at me. I allowed him his rage without returning anger. He immediately demanded that I go back to Paul who "is sad and mad and wants to be married to you." I hedged. "I am staying in the apartment. Dad and I are still angry. I still love David." Max was furious with me. Tonight, he and Andrew talked in bed. Max asked his little brother what he was going to name the toy bunny that David had given him. "Are you going to call it Debra or Steven, Max or Andrew?"

Tuesday, April 15

I've written a continuing series of angry, bitter epistles to David all night long. These are letters that I have no intention of ever sending. These are letters Charles Berman advises me to send to him—if I feel the need to mail off my words. So much anger, so much indignation, so much hurt.

A sampling:

As Gail Godwin wrote in *The Finishing School,* you have "congealed." Your choices are bad ones. I'm not easy, but I loved you completely and you turned your back to that for a place that was unloving and distant and even boring, but very, very familiar and safe. You'll regret your choice. But there may yet come a time when I do not.

If I choose to feel angry, I'm within my rights. You pressured me to tell Paul to put up or shut up. You pressed for separation last December and then called and yanked me back to you. You wanted me in this apartment, committed to you, waiting for you. You asked to marry me and then acted as though that all came from me.

If I were a lesser person, I would be plagued with my failings right now. I failed to keep this man I loved loving me. But instead I think, "You asshole—you blew the best thing that ever happened to you. Good luck, sucker."

You slunk back to your totally inadequate life and you will pretend to be happy for a while until you explode. And you had the audacity to ask where I would be in two years when that happens. David, oh David, there won't be another chance in two years; there never is. Your chance is now. Your lack of faith in us, in the love we had, your lack of commitment to me is devastating, but there it is and I can only accept it.

Unlike you, I can't roll out of bed with you and into bed with Paul. I'm much too loyal. Why is it that in sending you an angry letter, I know that—now you get to feel good and guilty—you get to wallow in that warm guilt you so love to feel?

Later in the Day

I'm making it through the day, but just barely. There are okay times followed by terrible times of yearning for David Muller—yearning for some sort of contact, any contact. I'm physically and spiritually needing him.

I awakened with pinkeye. My friend Frances said, "Yup, pinkeye, that's stress—and *Candida*, too." I looked *Candida* up—

"yeast infection"—and damn if I don't have that too. Stress. The last yeast infection was at the stressful beginning of the affair. So there you have it, when I want so badly to walk around looking good and sane and sound for the general public, I have a big red swollen runny eye and an itchy crotch. And then there is this constant lower back pain that began the very moment Paul told me David had moved back to Linda. The only other time in my life that I've had this backache was during the few days before I moved out of the farmhouse—it's totally psychosomatic.

Wednesday, April 16

What's David doing? It's Wednesday night and he's, of course, off work. What would I do if the phone rang and it was him? A few hours ago, after a two-hour phone conversation with my brother, Greg, I would have said with a laugh and a lilt, "David who?" and then, "What is it that you want?" I'd like to think that this pain and loneliness serve the useful purpose of moving me inexorably away from a doomed relationship. That's how I feel when I'm strong—each day, a bit farther from David Muller, from his self-deceit, his weakness, his competing need to control. And mostly, away from his inability to be analytical—a thing I've always recognized and appreciated as a welcome contrast to Paul's self-absorption and cerebralness. But because David isn't analytical, he was able to deny the call of home and family vehemently. He repressed and denied it until it surfaced against his will and then he said, "Maybe I don't love you enough."

So, if the phone rang now, nine days after I last rested my eyes on his wonderful face, touched his cheek and his fuzzy chest, would I have the strength to say, "Don't call me unless Linda knows, don't come to me unless you have divorced, don't touch me until you are certain it's me with whom you wish to build a future"? No, tonight, at this moment—if the phone rings—my entire body wants his entire body. I want so badly to make physical love with him. Yet, I also fear it. I cannot become only David's lover, his thing on the side—I know in my heart I cannot allow that to happen. Yet the loneliness and the physical and spiritual need to touch bodies and lives is overwhelming.

Thursday, April 17

I guess I'm hanging in all right. Maybe, just maybe, I will make it. But my moods are erratic and unpredictable, so I can't say for sure. Last night, I taught my classes, and damn it, I did an admirable job of it—pinkeye, sunglasses, and all. I gave the students a lot of time and a lot of me. I came back to this empty apartment—which is never easy—and read and slept for ten hours. I think that I'm coming down with some sort of flu. It's funny—the entire time David and I lived together, he had one sickness after another (obviously stress induced), but I was the picture of health. He'd get sick, the kids would get sick, yet I was strong and healthy and caught nothing. Now, the minute he walks out the door, I get pinkeye, a yeast infection, lower back pain; and at the moment, I feel feverish, dizzy, and head-achy.

I've been struggling just to get through the days—one at a time—keeping them full but not too demanding. It takes every ounce of my will and effort to avoid dwelling on the loss in my life. But always there remain blank spaces of time that automatically suck themselves full of the emptiness—the big black emptiness that David Muller has left. And in the big blackness, I see only the reflection of my own face—alone. And the face is filled with a terror that is unlike any other. Last night, I was dressing for class and I tripped into one of those empty spaces. I sat in the chair in my (formerly *our*) room, stared at the four-poster bed we've shared, and spoke out loud like a crazy woman to David for fifteen solid minutes. I spoke excruciating words of sadness and loss, as though he could hear me across the two miles to his home.

My friend Jack speculates that the dissolution of David and me hinged on the question of control. Jack, the son of a doctor, said, "It's the whole doctor thing—his need to control completely. He can do that in the big brick house on the hill and he can't do that in your home. He can do that with Linda, but he can't do that with you. In the big house on Long View Road, he controls the whole of his income (no alimony), he controls the wife, the kids, the animals, the job." Anyway you slice it, I can't do that for David.

Saturday I will go to Baltimore for a week's stay with my parents. I'm just trying to get to that, but I have no hope of comfort from my family. They see the breakup in such traditional terms—I somehow failed to hold on to this man. And then, after a week, I'll come back here to nothing—no plans, no person, no future—and that will be very hard. But I must take this a step at a time. Today, I write a bit, launder, pack, get sick a bit. Tomorrow, I get my hair cut, see Charles Berman, then go to Baltimore. That's as far as I can allow myself to look.

Friday, April 18
Today, for the first time in these three months I've been in therapy with Charles Berman, I cried my eyes out in his office. He said, "You're entitled."

He also freed me to write David in one week, "To set your mind at peace, to feel you've done all you can do, to let go." This has been my obsession, but I don't know whether I will write. I'm afraid of David's answer.

Monday, April 28, Morning
I've written an eleven-page letter to David describing the past three weeks. I don't know if I will mail it. Here are excerpts.

Dear David,
What I intend to write here, David, is the most honest, straightforward, unmanipulative collection of words of which I'm capable. If you asked my intent—what it is I want or expect of this letter—I couldn't answer. At one level, I want you to know, still again, what it is I feel, who it is I am. I know your enormous ability to convince yourself of feelings in others that are simply

not so. So, at this level, I want to be absolutely certain that you know the truth of me in these weeks we've been apart.

David, David Muller, nothing—nothing in my entire life—has remotely resembled the intensity of pain and loss I've experienced these past weeks. My abandoned book—the high-water mark, as you know, of personal suffering—becomes an amusing anecdote by comparison.

A few days ago in Baltimore, Susan, my friend, said to me, "You go back to a passionless marriage, or you step into the void." Well, David, it seems I have opted for the void. Undoubtedly, it was the same void you sidestepped just a couple days after you left that lone apartment key on the basement workbench here.

I've never been so alone, suffered such a loss, felt so afraid. In saying this, I'm aware of how easy my life has been until now, how much I've controlled the direction of it. I want you to know that my pain, hurt, emptiness, and loss have been acute. I want you to know, so that you *know*—not so that the knowledge will create guilt. I'm consciously, very consciously, controlling all instincts to go for your soft underbelly, to make accusations, to milk you of emotion. I will never again play tug-of-war for you—David Muller auctioned off to the highest emotional bidder.

There are times of strength David, don't think there aren't. There are times of acquiescence to the realities. There are times when I think we're saving ourselves from future pain. These times come and those who counsel in such things guarantee that all of this will get easier, that my life will get better.

But, David, that's a pipe dream now. In fact, there are no solutions I can expect for the extraordinary sadness and emptiness I've felt since you left my life. When I was with you in those early days, I sometimes felt that there were no happy endings, that it would be hard, no matter what. Now, as I sit here so very, very alone, David, where we used to be together, I know it will never again be as easy as it once was—as easy as it was to love you and be loved by you. I know that my life will be harder than it has ever been.

I haven't been able to return to Paul. I'm too filled with you, with my love of you, to reach out to Paul. The pull of Paul, another irony, is much less without you than with you. I can't allow myself the safety of that relationship—the congealment, if you will—of that marriage. I say that, David, knowing in a way that you cannot know, the absolute terror I feel of being single with two children to support and rear.

So, what have I told you and what have I not told you? Have I told you straight out that I love you? Have I told you how much pain your last note caused me—your telling me that I was "loved, cherished, admired, and respected" and then leaving me, with the finality of "always always always" being "remembered"?

Things have changed a great deal in these weeks. There are positions vis-à-vis you that I would never allow myself again. There is so much doubt—and trust, of course, has been dealt an enormous blow. But David, I love you, I feel empty without you; I've loved you these past six months, and I continue to.

Saying this to you may change nothing. But never will you be able to choose your course without knowing exactly what it is you have been offered.

Inette

P.S. Dave, Do you sleep peacefully in your bed at home? Do you awaken clear of head and heart? Are you a man who is contented with Debbie and Steve bounding into bed on Sundays, with Linda's kindness radiating, with gates to repair, a dog to bathe? Does the sense of serving your responsibilities soothe your worried brow? Does the warmth of being joyously welcomed back into the fold calm your confused and ailing heart? Do you ever allow yourself to wonder whether Inette is coping or thriving or withering without you?

I

Noon

I'm going crazy. I need to send the letter to Dave; I fear sending it. I'm certain it can change nothing for the better, that I will feel further rejected and humiliated. How much can I grovel for a relationship that even I see as doomed? But I can't seem to avoid acting. How can I flatter myself to think what I do makes a difference to what David does? How can he possibly leave Linda et al. after only two and a half weeks? I'm as driven and as scared as when I sent the note starting the affair. All day I've read and reread my letter, carried it around, sealed it, and still not mailed it.

Finally—one week late—I got my period today. What an incredible blow finding myself pregnant would have been! I've spent days thinking how I'd handle a pregnancy—my God, David's baby! What a bitter irony that would have been.

I am really feeling desperate, alone, empty. Berman isn't in yet. The kids, thank goodness, are not here. I am lost. I love and am not loved in return. Paul loves me and I seem unable to return his love. Is this some ridiculous adolescent charade? Where has my happiness of the past three months gone? Where does used-up happiness go? Is it a form of justice that Dave does to me what I do to Paul?

Three O'clock in the Afternoon

I mailed it. I sent David my letter, took it to the post office and put it in the slot. It will be in his hand tomorrow.

How many ways can he reject me? "I can't do that to Linda"; or "I love you, but not enough"; or "I'm sorry, Inette, Linda and I are moving to New Hampshire"; or "I'm happier at home, I'm at peace now"; or "You and I could never have worked, Inette." Will there be a phone call, a letter, or nothing?

My God, I don't want to continue feeling this pain. Will it ever be over? Will I torture myself by hanging on? I cannot kill myself—I *cannot* do that to my sons.

Midnight

In my distraction and madness, I try to distance my emotions, to objectify my feelings. Maybe it's bizarre, but it feels like therapy to write this story.

David Muller had cheekbones that defined the width of his beautiful face. He called his eyes "brown," as if that told you something. It was the way he described himself—inadequately, without recourse to introspection, and without particular insight. In fact, his eyes were not brown, not even nearly—they had a lot of yellow. And "brown" didn't even begin to describe their shape or size—they were very round, and wide-set, like the bones in his cheeks. And they were what marked his face as beautiful. His eyes could be shielded from views into his mind or as vulnerable as the day he was born. "Mrs. Muller's little boy," I'd say at such times. His eyes could also sparkle. They were most wonderful when they twinkled and shone at the top of his wide smile.

David Muller was German, Midwestern, and Lutheran—he was all three and yet none of the above. Jews mistook him for Jewish, and his mother attributed his intransigence in matters religious to "some Jewishness on the Snyder side." He was wildly attracted to things Jewish and urban and dressed in skirted business suits, with eyeglasses propped on top of long, curly hair. But he was essentially a boy with country tastes—most comfortable among mountains, with a gun in his hand, or alongside a trout stream.

David Muller was everything my husband was not and nothing that he was. I was everything David's wife was not and nothing that she was. That, of course, was the thirty-nine-year-old attraction. It was also what made it all seem very scary and very risky.

It was easy for friends and family to look at the intensity of David and Inette and the predictability of all the erratic moves we made and speak in cliches: "midlife crisis," or "adolescent hormones raging." It was very easy. And we made it easier by carrying on as though their words were water off a duck's back. We did exactly what pleased us. "Selfish, arrogant, and pompous" was what David's wife called him and my husband echoed to me. We'd laugh and say, "That's a match made in heaven."

We were, neither one of us, callous and unfeeling. No, neither one of us was that. David was filled with guilts about abandoned responsibilities and I was torn in parts by my sixteen-year love of Paul. But we each plugged into the other as the thing that would save us from extinction, and we wouldn't let go because we both knew once we did, the guilts and the fears and the social expectations would swallow us up and David and Inette would be lost to each other.

So we may have appeared "cruel," as one good friend accused, or precipitous, as everyone agreed when we announced our love of each other after only two months of Wednesdays. But we were simply holding tight to all that was fresh and lovely and loving in us. We saw the threats and the assaults from all sides. So we leaned into each other with our backs to the wind, and what looked like lack of feeling from the back was, in fact, the intensity of feeling for what we faced.

I guess there will come a time when I no longer love David Muller. I imagine, now that he's back home with his wife and children, that there will come a time when I look at what we were and nod along with the consensus that the relationship was flawed and could never have gone the distance. But right now, three weeks since the moment I last set eyes on him, six months since he touched my shoulder and told me, "I knew my life would never again be the same," I cannot imagine such a time.

It seems now as though David Muller, six months of David Muller right smack in the middle of my alloted years, will always shed his light on what came before him and all that comes after. I do love that man.

When we first made love, we did not actually make love. David was filled with his demons. But we did touch and talk and lie naked together. When we last made love, we knew each other so very well that there were no surprises but there was incredible eloquence; and Dave watched himself feeling, as though to memorize me and both of us to-

gether. God, can making love ever again be like that time
we each knew was the last?

Tuesday, April 29

Somewhere David sits in possession of my letter. It seems that
by now he must have seen it in his pile of office mail, and maybe
read it. I know that the letter can change nothing. It will be,
"I love you Inette, but I cannot . . ." and I will cry. But with
any luck at all, I'll begin to accept, really accept the end. I will
try to avoid hurt feelings, damaged pride, and the subsequent
angry letters to David. I'll try to avoid feeling demeaned and
rejected, but I can't guarantee how successful I'll be.

Wednesday, April 30

Dear Diary: Funny, I feel the impulse to start this entry like
that. This journal begins to feel like the same, never-ending
saga. David Muller just left. He was here for five hours (it is a
Wednesday). I cannot describe my euphoria at seeing his face
again, hearing his voice. I'm certain that I haven't seen the last
of him. I'm equally certain he cannot and will not leave his
family. "Family," he tells me, "is life itself. Family is like a small
republic; it has its own order and rules and institutions."

Tell me how I can counter that?

I did try. I laughed, I joked, I told him I loved him. He cried,
he laughed, he told me he loved me. He is the master of the
mixed message. Yes, he wants to see me. Yes, he wants to make
love to me. No, he is not happy in his home—he is miserable.
No, there is no question that he "prefers" me to his wife. And
there he sat with his wedding ring back on his finger. I hated
the sight of that fucking ring on his finger.

My conditions are only two. We can never make love while
he is living with his wife. He can never again move back into
this apartment—he would have to get one of his own. Other
than that, he's free to call me and come see me and I'm free to
write him since I cannot call.

He arrived bearing photos from our trip to Washington. He'd

just had them developed. There he stood at my door like an apparition from some wonderful past. What was stranger—the unreality of David's face in this apartment again or the photos of this happy couple arm-in-arm next to the National Gallery?

He sat on the sofa and I sat across the room on the rocker. Toward the end of his visit, he asked me to sit next to him on the sofa and I did, and we did touch arms gently and I did kiss his hand.

Thursday, May 1

He retreats to, "The family is life itself"—but his family is simply a parody of what life can and must be, to actually know you are alive. He is offered it all—the give and the take, the talking, laughing, crying, yelling—the incredible intimacy of some other one knowing all the ugly parts and *still* waking up in the morning and being ever so glad to curl up against you, to roll over and say, "I know you are self-centered, scared of what's inside you, sometimes self-loathing, but I love you, love it all, and I want you to do the same for me." And when he retreats to, "Family is like a small republic" and acts his role in the parody, he's so profoundly unhappy and unabsorbed by his life, so profoundly unused that he cuts grass with a vengeance and builds gates and runs and bikes and eventually settles into his old workaholic existence. And he *is* comfortable—"It is easy to go back," he says, because he's very sure of what to expect and what not to expect.

So maybe what he's saying is, "I need this particular republic because I know, really know, its laws and institutions, and in the other place—the one that offers so much—there's so much that's unknown and I'm scared."

In any case, he's already tasted a few of the rewards of the risks. He's already experienced the headiest of sensations—another human being who loves the very sight of him, the touch of him, and the smell of him. He has known just a bit of what it means to be consummately loved. And he knows that—for all the pitfalls, the fears, the risks—being loved and loving is an unquenchable addiction.

Saturday, May 3

I sit here and I find myself thinking that—despite the fact that I've seen David this week, written him three letters, felt his conflict and his love—he and I will most likely not make it. I know David is filled with feelings for me and I feel such joy with him, but I don't think our future lies together. And despite a real sadness attached to this notion, I am increasingly philosophical and personally stronger in the face of it. Still, I love Dave; still, I wish for a way clear of the morass; still, I wish there were a shortcut to his peace of mind—and mine.

Monday, May 5

This was a significant day. It was the first time I went out publicly in Watertown since David moved out. Today, I proclaimed to this incestuous little town that I still exist, I still survive, I look good, and I feel okay. It took every ounce of energy in my body to do it.

I spent five hours in the three-block area that is downtown Watertown, and that is no mean feat. I dressed to kill, walked tall, and talked. God, I talked. First to my lawyer, Sherry, ironing out the legal separation from Paul—how different that reads to me now, with no David on the horizon. On the first go-round, I worried about Paul's financial status and assumed my own would be well taken care of. This time around, there are my own economic needs to look after. Then, to lunch; then the rounds of the various shops and familiar faces. The point is that on this hot, sunny May day, I chatted, laughed, complained, and generally socialized for public consumption—*and* for my own need to face the music. And I am exhausted, but fuck, I did it!

Tuesday, May 6

I've been reading *The Writer and Her Work*, a collection of essays by some of my favorite contemporary writers—their thoughts on the juxtaposition of *writer* and *woman*. My God, they speak to me. Odd, in these recent years I have abandoned my identity as a woman who writes. How did that come to pass? Maybe I've never allowed myself the definition *writer*. Did that sound too pretentious, so I'd offer instead that I was a *journalist?* But you know, I believe that I am a writer, at least by instinct and temperament and interest. Whether I am a good, getting-better, capable-of-the-hard-work-of-it writer still remains to be tested. That's kind of exciting—the prospect of being tested at something this basic and this major—only one week shy of forty.

I think that teaching creative writing to other adults—serious people if not serious writers, people who are trying to work at it and enjoy talking about it and who defer to my pool of wisdom— has been a real flashing arrow for me. And I expect the book club last year—that collection of friends who wanted to read together—snapped me out of my somnolence and turned me back to thoughts of writing. My good friends knew something was askew these last years when I refused to face the necessity of my work. Then one year ago, I plunged two days a week into the intense work of a writing project—revision and more revision—for once, not simply the regurgitation of easy words. And I felt mighty fine about it. Then after six months' work, I sent it off, and with no other writing prospects in sight, I flew with wide open arms and soaring spirit into David Muller's life.

And *he* kept asking me throughout, "What is it that you want to do?" And I hated that he asked, because damn if I knew. I kept answering him, "It's been years of child rearing. Now I'll have to stumble around for a year or so to find my footing. I'll make wrong turns, try things that don't work, but I have to do that at this point." He never liked my answer and he kept asking me the same question.

So now he is gone and the creative writing class was simply wonderful, no other way to describe it—the give and take, the thinking and the talking about writing. But like the book club, like last year's still unpublished story, like this journal that has kept me writing these seven months (Lord, that's a lot of writing)—maybe like David Muller himself (gulp)—it has served my life's purpose. It's all part of this process of moving me back to myself as writer.

Do you realize that this is the first time in these seven months that I have written a journal entry that's not specifically and solely about the affair, the marriage, or the men? That may not be a writing accomplishment, but it is a therapeutic breakthrough, for sure. It's spring, my favorite month, and the warm Appalachian breezes are streaming in my open doors. Is it possible that I've learned nothing from the affair with David but everything from the loss of it?

Wednesday, May 7
David was here again this afternoon, this time for only one hour. He tells me that moving back to his home was "a gut thing, but the reasons of the intellect have caught up. It was the right thing to do." "Why?" I ask. "Because, otherwise, I would never have been able to put my ambivalence to rest, and now I can— but I must give my marriage more than three weeks," he says.

Am I allowing myself to be played with? I don't know. Am I kidding myself? Is my intense faith in us completely misplaced? "David, is this one big test?" Am I being tested at some incredible sport when I'm not even sure what the rules are?

I'm existing on some rocky shoals and nothing comes easily— not seeing David, not *not* seeing David, not assuming we are absolutely over, not thinking that we're too much in love to be anywhere near over. I sit and I think, "Does he want me to date and make him jealous? Does he want me to make a life elsewhere and take the pressure off him? Does he want me to wait faithfully? Does he want me to abandon hope?" He says one thing, he demonstrates another.

I ask him if he can take me out for my birthday, May 12. He says, "Sure, it has to be someplace very special." I say, "But how can you do it?" He answers, "I may just tell Linda. I can't stand that she walks around chirping so happily." So he's looking for blood. Why? To convince himself of emotion in Linda? So taking me to dinner for my birthday becomes a tool in David and Linda's agenda. Shit, that backache is back, that damn psychosomatic backache.

Thursday, May 8

The hardest, the very hardest thing for me to do is to wait. I can climb a precipitous mountain that I'm in no shape to climb—if I must. I can—if I must—tell a person in a position of authority that he's full of shit. I can spend time and kindness on a child. I can love and I can hate with great force. But it is physically impossible to wait on someone else's timetable—to wait now for David Muller to discover he needs and wants me, that he cannot live the rest of his life without me.

I feel constant panic, anger, frustration, and the surging of all sorts of emotions I am completely unable to control. Am I talking simple patience? Patience is a quality that Paul has painted in broad stripes up and down his spine. David doesn't have it—but he apparently also does not have my conviction. He isn't waiting, as I am, for the inevitable to happen—for us to be reunited. He's still working at this other thing, this marriage of his. He has a need to act through that scene, and intellectually even I know that must happen for him, for her, but mostly if there's ever to be an us again. Yet emotionally, I seem unable to wait. I make deals with myself—"You will not speak to him for two months," or, "You will not write to him." But I do.

Am I such an out-of-control child that I can't contain my simplest instincts? Is David Muller, of all the unlikely human beings in the world, teaching me lessons that Paul told me I needed to learn "scrubbing floors for two years in a nunnery"? I have never in my life waited on someone else's needs. Is that damn David Muller, of all the unhumble humans, teaching me humility? Is that son-of-a-bitch David Muller—of all the impetuous, impatient humans—teaching me patience?

And still I wait. It seems that I haven't a single choice in the matter. I wait because I cannot abandon the notion of David Muller and me together—I try, I will continue to try—but I cannot. So I say and feel, "You call all the shots," to David. And that is why I have moments of indescribable anger directed at that man—and indescribable panic about my prospects.

So I want to say, "I hate you, David Muller"; and I want to say, "I love you as I've never loved another living soul, David Muller"; and I want to say, "Fuck you, David Muller"; and I want to say, "Please, please, please, love me back, David Muller." I want to say it all and more—and all the while, I feel impotent. I feel impotent because my "hate" and my "love" and my "fuck you" and my "please love me" fall on ears deafened by their own blaring trumpets—listening, as we all do, to the orchestra of our own needs.

Friday, May 9

David called twice from the hospital last night. He was feeling the panic of being alone and we talked for hours. It felt like the old days, just carrying on, poking fun at him, and laughing. He talked more and more about the deficiencies of his marriage.

It was so normal, so right to be chatting at him and with him, but I couldn't sleep last night. After his call and his very candid admissions about Linda and himself, I can't imagine that we will not plunge ahead somehow. But, in saying that, I'm overwhelmed by the suffering that lies ahead—his fears, my fears, houses to sell, jobs, Linda, Paul, the children—days and weeks and months. Where does it begin and where does it end?

And that means completely relinquishing Paul—I'd forgotten how scary the relinquishing is—and David is right to hesitate. Today, sorting children's clothes and some books at the farm, I was reminded of the pain in relinquishing. For months now, I've agonized over comparisons between David and Paul: David doesn't have Paul's depth and self-analysis; Paul doesn't have David's energy, drive, and competence. But those comparisons are really beside the point. It seems I've made and then remade the same decision—I cannot help but choose David. Comparisons at some point are ridiculous—holding David up to a lifetime of missed qualities in Paul is absurd. You make your choice for whatever human and incalculable reasons, and that is all you can do.

Saturday, May 10

Sex. I believe that I cannot make love to David while he lives with Linda, and until his phone calls the other night, that seemed easy. But now, for the first time in a month, I crave him specifically. I imagine the explicit ways he touches me, the specific things he does to me, and it makes me crazy. I want to make love to him so badly, I hurt.

Andrew has begun a nighttime ritual of shrieking steadily for at least an hour at bedtime. It completely freaks me out. There is no time for myself, the children demand so much. It's much much harder facing the loneliness and frustration with Max and Andrew than without them. I vaguely remember being a good mother when David lived here, being a lousy one last fall during the affair, and now I'm an inadequate mother again. There's no one for *me* to draw on, and the children just pump it out of me.

I'm writing poorly, I'm being inexpressive. I can't seem to find the words tonight, it's all very diffuse. It's like the days before my period, only much more intense and wide-ranging—that same free floating anxiety. Maybe I just need a good cry. I haven't had one for two weeks—a real record. Earlier I was crying every three or four days, but it's very hard for me to cry alone—and right now there's no other person to cry on.

Sunday, May 11

Tomorrow is my birthday. David is taking me to the very posh and elegant Grove Park Inn, two hours away, for dinner. I'm very, very nervous. In some ways, the preparation (what *do* I wear?) feels like primping for an important date in high school. My fortieth birthday—is it part of the process of ending with David or is it part of our future? After my birthday, we have no other excuses to go out together. I'm putting together music—tapes—for the ride over. But what should the mood be? If I let myself love him and all he gives back is an evening out, how will I get through it? But I cannot hold back tomorrow—not on my birthday, of all days.

Monday, May 12, Morning

My fortieth birthday—I feel good, I look good, I even kind of like the number forty. Born in 1946, now forty in 1986; that's a lot of years. My brother wrote, "I hope your pain and sadness passes quickly. I know your next forty will be full of happiness and contentment." And right now, I believe that I will make them so. Here I am, in my own apartment, with my own bills, my own work, and my own money—caring for my children and myself. That counts for something. I am growing.

I look back on my thirty-ninth birthday, celebrated at a surprise party with a few friends (not one of whom still speaks to me), as the low point. Then I was at the end of a long downward spiral in activity, self-esteem, and personal growth. There seemed few possibilities one year ago. And Jack Benny, of course, ruined age thirty-nine for all of us—the dread anticipation of forty. But this year I have, at the very least, chipped away at the barnacles; penetrated the heavy mists I had been living in—and now, slowly, very slowly, at forty I will rebuild. At forty it all seems possible. It's not that forty is no big deal, rather it's a *very* big deal—a new beginning. Throughout this time I have felt that David is what I needed for that new beginning. Now I know that it will come with or without him.

Midnight

First there was an orchid corsage, then dinner at the hotel, then a wonderful cake David had ordered, and finally a tiny emerald and diamond pendant on a gold chain. What can I say about this evening? It was another magical evening with David Muller. I confronted him with each and every one of my doubts and fears, asked him every question I needed to have answered. He answered them all, one at a time, very patiently. I have decided to hang in there, to love him. He said he admired my strength and courage this past month. Whatever happens now,

I have had the most beautiful of fortieth birthdays—I have had my wonderful David at the lovely and quiet Grove Park Inn, and I have felt his love, if not his total commitment. I know how hard it is to choose, to pull apart from your previous life. I'm resolved to savor this evening of love and kind words and touched fingers, regardless of any disappointment that may follow.

Tuesday, May 13
   David just left—he was here three hours. He's removed his wedding ring again; he's moved out of his house into the hospital's call room. My God, we do love. My God, we do need one another. This is going to be the hardest thing I've ever done in my life, this trying to build a life with David. But my God, I want that, I want the rest of my life with that man. I want to fill in all his empty spaces, all his self-doubts; and he will respond with faith and faithfulnes—of this I am sure. Nothing from this day forward will be easy—nothing.
   We begin again with deceit and anger and legal things and unhappiness, and all I want is to be free to love my David and be loved by him.

Wednesday, May 14
   I sent this letter to David's office today.

   My dearest David,
   You cannot know how peaceful I've been since you left. There is in me a happiness, a certainty, a hopefulness, a lightness, a genuine serenity that I can't remember feeling before.
   This, despite the numerous imponderables—shrinks, an apartment, confrontations (painful, painful ones with Linda and Paul), anger and hostility, public and private attitudes, legal shenanigans, houses for sale, lives in limbo. I can list them, David. I can know in my heart and mind, and I look forward to none of them.
   But, my dear, dear Dave—I am in love and I am loved and

there is peace because I, too, feel we will deal with what we must to build our life together—that rich life of which you speak.

Each of the past three days, beginning with my birthday, you have said the things I needed to hear you say. Each day you have added to my security, detracted from my doubts. Each day, in your quiet, slow, earnest way, you have convinced me that I am central to your life, to your happiness, and to your future—as you are to mine. Tonight, at last, Dave, I'm calm, relaxed, at peace, quietly in love and dreaming dreams of you and me and our children together.

Inette

Saturday, May 17

There is this constant insecurity in the two of us: "Tell me what you feel at *this* moment." I feel like a bouncing ball. Why am I so unsure of David? How can I build a life where there's no trust? I'm very scared of what he just might do to me. Am I unfair? Is he faithful, loving, sure he wants me—or is he full of uncertainty?

Monday, May 19, Four in the Morning

This is going to be very hard. I do not feel like writing at all—I do feel like sleeping, but it seems that I cannot.

Last night David took his stand. He'd spent the day rereading my letters. Then he came to me, got down on his knees, and asked me to keep loving him, to be there for him. He had decided. He was terrified to leave his family, but he would. He would go to Linda immediately and tell her his decision. The next day he would find an apartment and go to the lawyer.

On his knees he begged my forgiveness for the hurts; he described the depth of his love; he promised a future in splendid detail. He positively glowed. He was happy and full of himself, full of love and committed. He had seized the initiative, and he was scared, but alive. He left for the hospital at nine P.M.

I went to bed at ten P.M. and awakened at midnight bolt upright, full of the certainty that David was talking to Linda, and I was scared. I lay awake for two hours feeling David's turmoil, but knowing that it was his—not mine—to deal with. At two A.M.,—five hours after he left me—the phone rang, and it was David. Voice drained, he said, "I have to come' over." He did.

"I cannot leave Linda and my children. I cannot make a life with you," he said. I made him describe what had happened. He told Linda he was leaving her, that he loved me, and he couldn't imagine a life without me. She demanded that the children be awakened and that he tell them his intentions. This David did. Steven sobbed hysterically, Debra clung to his leg and begged, "Daddy, don't leave me." He could not, he *cannot* do it. "Maybe some men can, but I cannot leave my family. I cannot."

I write now, two hours after he left. I have been bounced. It's all so classic—he couldn't leave his family, and I've left mine. Now I face the godawful loneliness again—how do I do it?! Will it be as bad or worse the second time? What the fuck do I do with my life? I've just called him at the hospital and said, "Don't worry, I'll be all right. I'm not angry and I don't feel betrayed. This is just life; that's all there is to it."

If Charles Berman should now ask me that question he has periodically recycled, "Would you do this again?" for the first time, I think I would have to answer, "No, I wouldn't do this again."

Seven in the Evening
The day is a blur. I've been very, very tired and yet unable to sleep. I went to the farmhouse with a cleaning woman to scrub it down for sale, simply following through the plans I'd set in motion last week. But I couldn't even speak to this woman—God only knows what she thought. I intimated inarticulately that I was getting sick. I tried calling Charles Berman all morning. He finally returned my call midafternoon and instructed me to get the hell out of that farmhouse, to go to the apartment, and to try to sleep. If I could not sleep, I was to call him. At

five P.M., I did. He repeated the words he spoke to me two months ago, "You might want to think about hospitalization. You need to get away from David and the kids for a few days." This time I listened. What other choice do I have? "I don't know, Charles, I don't know—what is this place, where is it?" He answered, "Hillsdale Psychiatric Hospital. It's new and attractive and people wear street clothes." And there was more he said, but I do not remember, I simply do not remember. "I'll think about it," I said, "then I'll call you back." I sat there in a puddle of grief, knowing full well I was completely unable to fix my own life, to care for my babies. A half-hour later, I called back. "What do I do? How do I get there? Will you check me in, Charles?" He told me to pack and to find someone to drive me the two hours over the mountain roads to Asheville. There is no one to drive me," I said. "I'll drive myself—I'll be fine." But I wasn't at all sure that I would be. I called Paul, who has had the children since yesterday, told him where I would be "for the next few days," and asked him to take care of our children. Two hours later, I'm packed and on my way.

Part V
PIECING TOGETHER

Tuesday, May 20

Yesterday was the most extraordinary day of my life. Last night, in the pouring rain and the pitch black, alone, I navigated my station wagon for two hours over the winding mountain roads to this place. I carried my weighty suitcase up the front steps of this building and waited for someone to open the locked doors. I asked to be admitted to the Hillsdale Psychiatric Hospital— and I was very scared.

Still I remain uncertain why I have done this thing. But I know that my hopelessness is so acute, my distress so extreme, my fears of being alone so terrifying, my depression so overwhelming that for the first time in my life I can neither sleep nor adequately function awake. I can imagine *no* life without David, no life unmarried, no life alone with my two children.

The hospital, the feelings. So what's a nice girl like me doing in a place like this? Of course, everyone else here is crazy, but not me, right? Last night, I felt certain that I'd overreacted in coming here. Obviously Dr. Berman was instrumental—but the decision was mine.

I see people here talking on phones. I think that there's no one in my life to call from this place. Who would want to hear from me? Who would I want to call? So that's what I've done to my life. Paul tells me that we're all ultimately alone. Yes, yes, yes—the basic human condition, I know all about that. But when you check yourself into a psychiatric hospital, when you drag your heavy suitcase to the locked doors, when nurses meticulously search through your belongings and confiscate your bottles (of makeup); your aerosol cans (of deodorant); your scissors, tweezers, hair dryer, eyebrow pencil sharpener ("It has a razor," the nurse explains patiently), dental floss (to hang myself?); when all doors leading to the sunlight are sealed, when you have voluntarily put yourself in such a place—you know, *know* that you are shrieking out loud, "My life is shit—*Help* me!"

Do I go public with this? I have with almost all else. Do I tell the world where I am? Is that a part of this experience—a public statement of being overwhelmed by the events of my life?

I keep feeling compelled to make silly jokes about this place. "Please," I laugh, "no arts and crafts for me, no basket weaving"; or, "Yes, I'll guard these scissors with my life." It is bad, self-protective, manic humor.

The place, despite the best of intentions, is a hospital. It's small; all rooms are on one floor; the halls are wide; the rooms are spanking new and cheap, motel-room sterile. The gym looks remarkably barren and uninteresting.

Lounges are the center of the activity-less activity—half are smokefree, half (the fuller ones) are smoke filled. All have huge televisions and pseudohealthy snacks (Coke with no caffeine, cubes of American cheese). No one touches the shelves of dated, but not classic books (my suitcase was leaden with my books). There are daily newspapers for which I'm grateful, a sundeck that's locked, and a "dining room" that is in fact a cafeteria.

Of course, I'm still alone here. I ate breakfast alone and studied the faces of the other patients. No one here for me, I decided—not my kind of people. Who are these people and why are *they* here? So I'm dressing to assert my status. (I lack only a badge and bracelet of keys to be staff.) I asked Charles Berman before I packed, "What clothes will I need in a mental hospital?" He laughed and answered, "They're all naked and chained to the walls—you won't need a thing." Always, I try to impress—I stand straight, look people in the eye. Always, I assert my class—let the world of patients and staff know that there's no ordinary redneck here, no ignorant lout here. So nothing really changes. Or maybe that's what this place is about—everything changes or will. I charm the staff with my wit. My God, clearly they've seen it all before, so I kid only myself. In time, of course, I'll know these people and they'll have some insights into me.

At this moment I'm feeling claustrophobic. Thank God, Charles Berman is down the hall doing his thing and will meet me within the hour. I'll be able to share my feelings with my one "friend" (paid, I know) in this place. I'm feeling the extreme closedness of the place. I can't get it out of my mind. I've walked and rewalked—practically run—the limits of this floor, so I'm very aware of the parameters of my physical life here; and at this moment, I'm hating it.

7:30 P.M.

I've done it. I've gotten through my first almost twenty-four hours in a psychiatric hospital, and I'm still here to talk about it. My suspicion is that all of what appeared very strange this morning becomes more and more normal. Still, I'm blissfully alone in my double room. There are no private rooms here because patient interaction is a big part of the therapy—they want no one isolating herself. My room is in the geriatric unit (all old people) because the adult unit is completely full and because I begged Charles Berman for a private room. Am I isolating myself or do I just appreciate the quiet space to read and write?

A young therapist took my social and emotional history this morning, and out of nowhere I cried and said, "Paul and I were virgins when we met. I'd never considered being unfaithful. Our union was sacred."

Then to lunch and my first conversations with other patients.
"You don't seem like the sort of person who would be here,"
one young man said to me, confirming my carefully held supe-
riority. But another young man looked me straight in the eye
and asked, "So, are you depressed?" Right to the point.

This afternoon I went outside—hallelujah! I picked honey-
suckle for my room, walked around in the sunshine, looked at
the mountains, and smelled the fresh-cut grass. God, I needed
that. Now, because Berman okayed the official grounds pass, I
can go wherever I wish—at half-hour intervals, when someone
unlocks the door for me, when I sign in and out, when I carry
a bright yellow pass, if I cross no streets, and when it's not dark.
How's that for freedom?

My first group therapy today was Assertiveness Training. "Me!
Assertiveness Training?" I asserted to anyone who would listen
and fought the idea in typical Inette fashion. Charles Berman
answered, "In some sitautions with David you haven't been assertive, you've been passive. In some situations with Paul you
haven't been assertive, you've been aggressive." I guess I'll come
to understand the distinction.

Assertiveness Training is a large group, about twenty-five, led
by cute, blond Dr. Joe Wylie, a psychologist. "He's about our
age," Berman described Wylie. In fact, this Dr. Wylie reminds
me so much of Ed, my friend of fifteen years in Cleveland—the
way he leans his chair back on its hind two legs and straddles
it, the hand gestures, the word patterns are Ed's. So it's hard not
to see Joe Wylie as a peer. Of course, Wylie is the doc and I'm
the patient. The group is intellectually challenging, as teaching
my writing courses was this winter—making my mind and my
words work. The *emotional* challenges lie ahead. Everyone refers
to Psychodrama as the biggie. One patient described Psychodrama as the equivalent of running twenty-six miles and "hitting
the wall" with exhaustion. Today fifteen people poured out of
Psychodrama sobbing.

I met another of Charles Berman's patients today. Connie is
from a larger town, one I know well, about an hour from my

farm. She sat next to me in Assertiveness and I immediately picked up kindred-spirit feelings, wit, and intelligence. I had dinner with her later. She arrived here on Mother's Day, is thirty-six, has been married fifteen years, and has two children, ages fifteen and eleven. She's good looking and athletic (she has a great body). We didn't exchange stories, only our ideas about this place. After dinner she introduced me to a Black woman named Margaret from a small city near here: about thirty, also nice and bright, divorced with two small children. She promptly volunteered to show me the bullet wound in her shoulder, chortling as she did that she took so many pills before she shot herself that her aim was terrible. So these people become interesting, real, and I already look forward to knowing them.

Drugs. Antidepressants are an essential part of the therapy here. Three times a day there are "med lines." An announcement over the public address system summons the patients to the nurses' station to await pills. The pills must be swallowed in front of the attendant. My big fear of psychiatric hospitals was drugs. Before I agreed to come, I told Berman I would not take antidepressants. He assured me he was very conservative and that I had the last word. He's prescribed no drugs for me and I've taken none. He had an optional sleeping pill awaiting me the night I arrived; I did not take it.

Tonight I ran two miles around the gym. I eat a lot here—"just to sit in a different room for a while," as Connie says. Everyone gains weight here—every Tuesday, they pull a big scale out into the hallway, rally the team, and weigh us in. So I run to counter the fat, the boredom, the unexpended energy. After adult gym time, the adolescent patients pour into the gymnasium. These kids fly in and are all over the floor—very much like bees swarming a hive—all over the place, humming and buzzing. And I think I have unexpended energy!

It's been quite a day. So far, the staff is impeccable, simply impeccable. I cannot criticize a thing. They're sensitive, caring, intelligent, respectful, and studiously unobtrusive. My five months of Friday outpatient sessions with Berman have been "crisis therapy," he said. "Here, they'll prepare you to deal with it all over the long haul." I'm here, he said, because I need to be away from David and the kids. So I get a peculiar sort of break. "It ain't the Bahamas," Berman said.

Wednesday, May 21

I got through the night, but not with style. There were bad times, craziness, midnight and two A.M. angry phone calls to Paul. There were four aborted calls in all, two he hung up on— ugly destructive words. The staff came into my room and let me talk, talk myself through the night.

I just met Dr. Badgely, Berman's partner. He's very direct and concrete where Berman is more circumspect and nonconfrontational. "Yours is a classic forties crisis," Dr. Badgely said. "I see two of these a week." He too is emerging from one. "For six months," he said, "your life will be the pits. At nine months, you'll be out of it, and in one year you'll be ready to form another relationship."

Thursday, May 22, six A.M.

I called my parents last night to tell them where I am. Obviously, it was a bolt of lightning. In the whole of their lives they never considered that one of their children would call and say, "Hold onto your hats, I'm in a psychiatric hospital." My mother reacted characteristically: "But *what* will you do when you get out?" she grilled me. "You have got to fight it, Inette." My father, bless his heart, interrupted and said, "I think you're doing the best thing, I'm proud of you." Support comes from where you least expect it. But it all becomes crystal clear who programmed me in the fight-the-bad-feelings department.

After my terrible night Tuesday, last night I slept a full eight hours. What a difference sleep makes. Here, when you say you've had a rocky night's sleep, everyone is full of empathy—staff will say, "Oh I'm so sorry," or "I hear you had a bad night"; and patients nod knowingly, maybe make a joke or maybe say a few words that assure you they've been there. Much ado about sleep.

8:15 A.M.

I'm feeling really up right now. I've just spent two hours so-cializing with a bunch of men—patients on the drug and alcohol unit—nice ego-stroking socializing. I'm thinking that for years I've been stultifying, unchallenged, not growing. And I know these weeks here will be an enormous shot in the arm, head, and rear end. I'm a minute away from the much-discussed Psy-chodrama. I'm excited and fearful. In a way, this is a spa, an intensive college course, a total immersion in growth and change, and I love the idea. Whether I love the emotional reality remains to be seen.

10:10 A.M.

Psychodrama is quite extraordinary—the feelings, the empa-thy, our sensitivity to one another are remarkable. It's a lovely group. Susan Lewis, the staff leader who "directs" the drama, is a real pro. There are four adolescents among ten adults in the group—girls who have been raped or abused in one way or an-other. Despite their extreme circumstances and my relatively sheltered adolescence, the very sight of these girls brings back all the horror of adolescence. I didn't even want to touch these girls, but I forced myself to. Their awkwardness and extreme discomfort are undoubtedly reminders of my own continuing adolescent insecurities. Susan Lewis said she thought her thirties were "a chance to relive my adolescence and do it right this time." I like that.

Psychodrama is acting out, in play form, some aspect of a person's life. The patient doing his psychodrama selects where and when the action takes place, describes the scene, and selects the other patients to play the central characters in his life. The director, Susan, moves the drama along with rapid-fire sugges-tions and dialogue. The lights are turned very low and the scene is set and reset with the rearrangement of furniture and other props. There are many patients who vehemently refuse to partake in Psychodrama because of the violent noises that escape from behind the locked door. In fact, foam bats are beaten, pillows are pummeled, patients get tackled, there are blood-curdling screams. Central to this therapy is the physical acting out of feelings. It's the only place here where my verbal proficiency is of no advantage at all. It's all feeling—anger, grief. Each psychodrama lasts two hours.

3:15 P.M.
Cute Dr. Wylie's Assertiveness Training. I talked about being afraid of being outside of a relationship. We agree that inside a good one is best, but it's okay to be on your own, to know that you can do for yourself and not feel panicky dependency.

Each patient has a schedule card. At 8:30 there is Psychodrama; at 10:30, Group; at 1:00, Assertiveness; then Stress Management and Biofeedback, and Cognitive Therapy or Aerobics; Leisure Management, Volleyball, and Arts and Crafts. The patients, oddly enough, call these sessions "classes." To some degree you choose your activities, to some degree you don't. I elected no Arts and Crafts. There is little free time and because each day's schedule is different, I'm constantly referring to my card to see where I must be.

Berman made a reference to discussing me in a "team meeting." It turns out that once a week, all my therapists sit down together with Charles and pool their insights about me. What do they say? I'd love to be a fly on that wall.

Friday, May 23
I played volleyball last night and all I could think about was an old Woody Allen routine describing a manic-depressive volleyball game, and I kept grinning and chortling to myself. There's no killer instinct in this game—good and terrible athletes alike fumble around congratulating each other on even the most horribly botched shots. I told another patient my Woody Allen fantasy and she laughed and said, "Every time we line up in the med line, I see Jack Nicholson in *One Flew over the Cuckoo's Nest* stashing pills in his cheek."

Dr. Berman confided to me this morning that he got a phone

call last Tuesday from a Dr. Muller in Watertown—purportedly about a patient referral. Berman refused the call and refused to return it. He said he won't be David's messenger to me. So, David called Charles's office—what a thing for him to do. How did David know I was here? Only Paul knows and I asked him to tell no one. Berman's assessment is that David wants it all—his family and me on the side. There is *no* way I can be bounced again, my dear, dear David. David needs extensive therapy just as I do. He can't work this out alone, but he rejects help. Therapy is probably the only way he can find the answers—for me, for Linda, but mostly for himself. And because I love him—and I do—I want that for him, just as I want this for me.

It's been a busy day. This morning was a good aerobic workout in the gym, as strenuous as my Jane Fondas, and it felt good. Then on to my first group therapy. The psychologist, Dr. Cannon, is a woman about thirty-five, very blond and pretty and "dressed for success." There are six patients and this Dr. Cannon is very on top of the interaction.

Then comes Community Meeting. Once a week, the staff and the patients sit down together and bitch at one another. It's the one opportunity for the patients to affect the rules and the bureaucracy of the place. I said, "I want the sundeck unlocked so I can work on my suntan." Obviously, it wasn't a big issue. But a far more heated one was whether patients' children could be permitted to visit our rooms. The discussion was very very emotional. There's not a woman here who doesn't carry a heavy burden of guilt for being here—and, in a sense, abandoning her children. The kids miss their mothers, are confused, and, if older, are often embarrassed that their mothers are here. The patients are insisting that children be allowed inside rooms—to demystify the psychiatric hospital and allay their children's terrors—to show them where their mothers live. Hillsdale has so far prohibited this for some vague and always changing reason. Terry was absolutely brilliant on this issue and she appears to have won some allies on the staff.

Then I go on to Wylie's Small Group or, more properly,

Cognitive Therapy. This session joins five hand-picked patients for what Wylie calls "individual therapy in a group setting." There's a certain cachet to being included in this group. My perception is that the more educated and verbal patients find their way into Wylie's "Small Group." Wylie told me that I remind him of Lily Tomlin. Lily Tomlin, can you imagine? She's only about my favorite performer. "Really?" I asked, "but I'm not funny." He said, "Yes, you are." I *am* funny with David but never with Paul. Are there many things my marriage with Paul doesn't permit?

In each of my groups there's one person being discharged tomorrow. They all look so healthy and happy—kind of cured. They, we all, love this place and the people here. Isn't that an amazing thing to say?

Midnight

This evening I had my first severe anxiety attack—at least, the first one that I could label. I was running laps outside on my grounds pass when it suddenly hit me. I realized the obvious— David knew I was here because Paul had called and told him. Husband Paul dumping garbage on lover David—the two of them exchanging bits of sympathy and gossip about *me*. The thought makes me crazy. Connie and her good friend Kathy saw me come back from my run all agitated, depressed, and generally freaking out—they guided me into my room, sprawled out like college coeds on my bed, and talked me through it. They've been there; and they lavished me with their warmth, their total attention, and their good sound advice. We went on for hours until I eased up a bit. Thank God for Connie and Kathy.

Kathy, in her mid-forties, is street smart. She's been a labor organizer and a Democratic Party functionary—an old-fashioned liberal. She's had more awful things happen to her than any human being deserves. Her first husband was brain damaged in a car wreck when she was pregnant and he subsequently died. She's been raped, her second marriage ended in divorce, and she managed to rear three children well, without any support. She calls her life a "bad novel." But none of that sent her to a psychiatric hospital. For the past ten years she's lived with Bob, a very bright engineer who never actually got around to divorcing his wife. At forty-five, Kathy realized she was giving more to the relationship than she'd ever get back from Bob, that he would never marry her—and the depression that followed ended with hospitalization. Kathy is the funniest woman I know—very, very clever. Damn, I want her to make it.

Connie is also remarkably funny, but her humor is more self-protective. A few nights ago I told these two women the story of my affair and Connie got this look on her face and started sobbing. "I'm not the only one," she said, "I just heard you say you had an affair, too." Connie, Catholic and married to a certified public accountant, is a scrupulously devoted mother. She's tormented with guilt over her affair, wants desperately to remain in her marriage, and is dealing with an unforgiving husband and her own self-hatred.

Connie, Kathy, and I seem to have quickly cemented a friendship. In the midst of the heartbreak and unhappiness of this place, we are three women who laugh an awful lot.

Saturday, May 24
My first weekend pass: I left the hospital grounds for the first time since I arrived Monday night to go to the bank and cash a check—and it wasn't easy. I dawdled in the lounge, talking, to avoid going out. There was a barrier of fear to leaving the place. Kathy and I climbed into my Ford station wagon with the kids' seats, and I told her about my lonely drive over the mountains to Hillsdale. "You came alone?" she repeated, amazed. "You *are* gutsy." Almost all patients are driven here by famiily, friends, or the police. It felt like years—not five days—since I was behind the wheel driving, and I was timid. So this place that aims to build your confidence and self-esteem also fosters a certain dependence (on rules, on someone else to care for you and structure your days). I was afraid to venture out and do the things I've always done with ease. My God, what does it take to climb in

a car and direct it where you want, hop out, and do what you
need to do?

Connie talks about feeling that everyone *knows* you're a patient
of the Hillsdale Psychiatric Hospital, out on a pass—that you're
"one of the crazies." I did feel like Exhibit A.

Sunday, May 25

I'm physically beat. Yesterday I went to the May Festival with
Kathy and her family and it was all too much—the crowds, the
heat. None of it was pleasant and I was glad to come back through
these doors. I wish that the weekend were over and I could get
back to the business of therapy. I saw several patients and their
families at the festival yesterday, and they all looked very different from me. Funny, here the differences melt out in the
similarity of feelings, but out there, the social and economic
chasm is stark. A psychiatrist I don't know came in today covering for Charles. He asked about yesterday's pass and I told him
that it was awful. "Get out there again today," he ordered. "Passes
are part of the therapy. This is a very controlled environment,
and *that* out there is the real world. Keep your eye out there."
He wished me a better day.

Seven P.M.

I just stood on a chair in front of the little bathroom mirror
over the sink to get a look at my naked body. There are no full-
length mirrors here (a fact that Connie's fifteen-year-old son
immediately noticed), so I have taken the state of my lower
body, until this moment on faith. Well, my body still looks all
right.

Here are some random thoughts. My favorite Connie phrase
is, "We were singing from different songsheets." I love it. It
perfectly describes the missed connections in human relationships. My favorite Inette phrase is, "This place is an acquired
taste." And it is. The enclosing and the nurturing are very different from the hostility and threats of the outside world, but
you do have to open yourself to the possibilities here.

The other night Kathy talked about my losses. "Inette, you've lost your husband, your family, David, your social position." My losses—heavens, we are all here suffering losses. My self-respect, there's a loss; my confidence, there's another.

In the lounge just now, a woman named Beth talked about the expectation that she always be strong. "And I *am* strong," she said, as her hands trembled and she could barely get the cigarette to her lips. "But I'm grieving." Beth is an artist who makes architectural stained glass. The other night she walked through several of her larger windows and smashed them to pieces, escaping major injury. Her husband of ten years left her for another woman. She has suffered an abortion and two subsequent miscarriages and desperately yearns for a child. She's in her late thirties.

Having temporarily won the battle for my solitary room, I begin to understand why it's therapeutically important to be with other patients.

Monday, May 26, Memorial Day
Have I written a true description of this place? Have I written about the people sitting at the breakfast table with their heads in their hands? Or about people standing in med line sobbing about children who blame themselves for the fact that mommy's in the hospital? Or about patients staring despondently into the empty distance mumbling about "last Memorial Day?" Have I written about the many, many desperately sad people who surround me? How anyone who isn't sad at the moment is a shoulder to cry on?

I just had an hour session with Charles Berman. We talked about my search for the man who has everything to fill the big vacuum of confidence I have in myself—that, and my all-or-nothing approach to things and people. I'm the best writer or I'm no damned good as a writer. David is the love of my life or nothing. All or nothing.

I was able to finally answer Berman's two-week-old question—what originally attracted me to Paul. It was his incredible sweetness, kindness, and generosity. Berman, always the advocate for the marriage, answered typically, "There are not many people like that."

We talked about my mother, who essentially tells me to "fake it," implying that I don't have "it," and my father who tells me he'll pay my way—"take care of me"—implying that I can't do it myself. Still, Berman says that I have the unconditional love of both of my parents, which is far better than most of the patients around here. It appears I'm looking for the man that my father was when I was seven or eight. Until I fill my own spaces and self-doubts, I can't form a relationship with Paul, David, or anyone else. So there it is, the crux of it all and what Paul has said all along.

What a place this is. I write in the central lounge, the one no one ever uses because there's no smoking, it has no television, and it's in full view of the nurses station. People really do leave you be in this hospital. Of course, the staff works at being unobtrusively ever present. The patients are great respecters of each other's space. I feel very public—writing in this glass-walled lounge, for the first time outside of my own room—in full view. Hell, this is what I do, they know it, they may as well watch it happen.

Tuesday, May 27

Biofeedback was a kick. It's all about relaxing. The machine measures blood pressure, skin sensitivity, heartbeat, and all the physical measures of relaxation. I sit and watch the graph that measures the degree of my tension on a computer monitor. I think "David Richard Muller," and the line on the monitor shoots off the chart, disappears completely from the screen. Then I consciously and with some effort use my natural-childbirth breathing techniques and make myself relax. "At least this shows you *can* relax," Dr. Pedrozo said as the line reappears on the screen. "It gives you a sense of power." I said, "I could use a little of that right now." It's a good tool.

Beth talked at lunch. "The men here are very sensitive men

who don't live in worlds that allow them that and they don't know how to deal with it. The women here are women who love very deeply and completely. Ninety-five percent of the women in the adult unit are suffering from a broken heart." I find her description apt. The women here are largely suffering from depression stemming from some flawed marriage or affair of the heart. Beth said, "When I immerse myself in my art, I don't know where I'll come up but I know that I will. When I immerse myself in loving a man, I don't know that I will come up."

10:30 P.M.

Paul and the boys came to visit this evening. The Community Meeting bitching bore fruit, and they were allowed inside my room. Paul's reaction to the place was intense—through his eyes it all looks very institutional, through his eyes the patients look peculiar. He was a bit freaked and I'm glad. He's been so casual about my being here and now he knows a little bit of the reality of my life. But, unfortunately, watching his reaction does bring that reality back to me.

I packed Styrofoam lunch boxes full of dining room goodies, such as sugar packets, small cereal boxes, and plastic utensils for the boys. It was Connie's idea to make gift boxes for them and they were thrilled. What presents can you give children from a psychiatric hospital? Max brought me treats from his kindergarten graduation, which I missed today. Andrew was gravitating to Paul—that's where his attachment is now. It makes me feel sad and inadequate. This baby of mine is feeling abandoned, and I feel guilty—still more guilt. We went out on a pass for pizza and frozen yogurt. Max wanted to know when I would be home; my answer was vague, and he cried as the car pulled away. I did, too.

Am I unreliable to those boys? I don't feel better able to care for them now than when I came in. Poor little Andy, it's so hard to reach out to him now. He needs to be nurtured and I'm not doing it. Max verbalizes his demands for attenton, and still I don't do it. I really feel that I'm failing at something I care a great deal about.

After the visit, Connie, Kathy, and Beth homed in on me. They wanted to feel—not just know—how it went and they were so kind and considerate of me. In a way, I'm glad Paul and the boys are gone, and I can return to my normal life here (I'm not unaware of the irony)—unobserved by outsiders. I'm glad they came and I'm glad they left. I want my peace here.

Kathy said that she feels a lot of hostility for Paul in me. She may be right, but about what and from where, I don't yet know. Dr. Wylie said in Assertiveness, "An affair is an act of aggression in a marriage." And Connie's primary therapist told her, "There's always a reason within the marriage why an affair starts." I think about my anger toward Paul and I think about all of his emotional secrets from me. He's always held back his feelings, shared all his thoughts, but few of his feelings. *Still* he's full of his secrets— I hate secrets. I hate that I can't make him open up to me and yet he depends on my emotional openness, on my lack of secrets.

Wednesday, May 28

They put a roommate temporarily into my solitary room. Connie calls her a "fruitcake." There are patients here who insist she's a direct retaliation for my wanting a private room. She's a woman in her early thirties who walks very slowly, speaks not at all, snores, and is exceedingly ugly. But I guess she's unobtrusive, as things go. Some nurse came in this morning and told this woman that she has a "great roommate. Inette keeps us all laughing, she's our therapy." Well, who could imagine? You take your positive strokes where you get them.

As I sit here and write, "hostile Sarah" (as opposed to "quiet Sarah") comes in and lays all her stuff on me. Everyone steers clear of her. She's very young, maybe nineteen, barely qualifying for the adult unit. She's incessantly full of her own story. She's angry at the world. On a good day I can put my arm around her and mother her, but right now she's just an intrusion.

Next Coco bops in and gratuitiously tells me she was sobbing last night because my boys were here and reminded her of her own boys, whom she hasn't seen since Christmas. Coco holds the longevity record here—four months. This is a short-term facility and the average stay is three to four weeks. Coco is the classic adolescent apple polisher, but twelve years past adolescence. Once I walked to the lounge barefoot and she officiously warned me that I would get in trouble for being shoeless. I answered, "What are they going to do, send me to a mental hospital?"

Finally, as I sit in my room with my door open and try to write this, a very mean, six-foot, four-inch Black man stops by wanting to "come up to Watertown and pass some time" with me. He's been frightening women on this floor for three days now. I'm not sure if that's because he's Black or that's because he's big and mean.

Why is this afternoon such a zoo? My zombie of a roommate wanders in and out, sipping off big plastic bottles of Diet Coke, and the rest of this moderately crazy world weaves in and out.

10:10 P.M.

The patients are militant now. They're passing a volleyball petition. After the other night's spirited game, there were three or four injuries (all contracted benignly in search of a point). So the administration halted volleyball. What they failed to take into account was that, around ten P.M., patient energies hit a high and are in dire need of an outlet. The juices right now are running full steam and the outlet of the moment is this opposition group and its petition.

Thursday, May 29

This was quite a morning. Terry acted out her story in Psychodrama. Terry is an angry and aggressive woman of large stature, but she's also a natural nurturer—everybody's mother. She and her husband have a twelve-year marriage that is fueled by their mutual hostilities. The usual excuse for battle is their sons. Today in Psychodrama Terry vented her anger toward her husband, who whacked their son, and toward her father, who repeatedly beat her.

I was her alter ego. I played her with great, great, anger toward both of those men, and I truly don't know where my anger came from. I screamed at her husband for his irrationality; I screamed and beat that bat against the wall with murderous rage; I yelled and I hit and I don't know why. I was eager to assume Terry's anger, very eager, and I did one hell of a job. But why?

This marriage of mine needs examining. I'm opening myself on all other issues but I'm refusing to go at this marriage and I must.

Berman, in my team meeting, suggested I leave the hospital after only two weeks. "Your answers aren't going to come in four or five weeks, but over the long haul of outpatient psychotherapy. This is crisis relief," he said. The rest of the team insisted I needed two more weeks. Connie was told that she will leave one week from tomorrow. I can't imagine being here without her.

Eleven P.M.

The dynamics of this place continue to amaze. (1) Beth got a pass today—dressed in business suit and earrings, she marched off to her lawyer's office to confront the outrageous financial demands being made of her by the hospital's business office. One arm of the machine seeks to cure her and the other creates incredible stress. The business office backed down. Hurray! (2) Kathy confronted her primary therapist in front of her psychiatrist and got a change of "primaries." Hers had been giving her the short shrift. Hurray! (3) Terry is requesting a change of shrinks— a huge step—and taking action to get herself admitted to Wylie's small, elite, Cognitive group. Hurray! (4) Volleyball is back on the agenda after the petition and general griping. Assertiveness breeds assertiveness. I'm so proud of my friends here.

We feel at times very women's-groupish, very feminist, very healthy. We all run laps around the gym—making jokes about the place, stroking our collective ego and feeling very good about ourselves. This must be healing.

The adult unit houses twenty-five patients. Maybe five of them at any given time are men. On the same floor there are a similar-sized geriatric unit, a drug and alcohol abuse unit that is heavily male, and an adolescent unit. There is also the neutrally named Unit Four, which is the lockup for violent admissions. I was here a week before I knew it existed. It sits at the end of the adult unit hallway, but the glass windows are shaded. Patients in the adult unit love to wallow in paranoid fantasies of being shunted to the dreaded Unit Four for misbehavior. In fact, the big Black man is now in Unit Four. Beth began her enforced tenure (she was committed after she walked through her stained glass) by spending two days in Unit Four. She said the rooms are tiny singles, cigarettes are held by the nurses and doled out, and there is absolutely nothing to do. Obviously the patients are heavily sedated.

Friday, May 30

Wylie's Cognitive group was mine today. Wylie began, as always, by asking all of us to relax. It became immediately clear by my crossed ankles and stiffly held neck that I could not. He asked, "What do you fear will happen if you relax?" and I answered, "Exposure." "Of what?" he asked, and I said, "of my weakness." "Why?" he asked and I answered, "Because I'm supposed to be strong." "Says who?" he asked, and I said, "My mother." And that's where it started.

My tension, my inability to relax, to act spontaneously, my need to control are all my mother's heritage. This is the mother *inside of me* who, in all of my forty years, I've not separated from. I have never acted independent of this woman who is my loving mother. I have always reacted to her or acquiesced to her. "Oh, you rebel you," Wylie laughed at the end of the session. Mine have consistently been acts of rebellion, never of independence.

So in Cognitive, I argued my case to my mother and she argued her case to me. I discerned the differences, acknowledged and accepted them. The self that is me won the day. "Mom, I'm *not* you, I'm different—I love deeply, feel a lot, make friendships, need people. I'm sorry that I'm not the same as you, but I'm not rejecting you. Mom, I can't 'fight the feelings' because it makes me tense and unhappy." My mother is controlled and has enormous difficulty expressing the love she undoubtedly feels. She can't reach out for genuine friendship outside of the family, she can't relax or allow herself to be vulnerable—but that is not me.

After dinner, two people from my Cognitive group told me that I have "a glow." Funny, I'm not even smiling my usual smile, yet I have a glow. I can feel that my face is loose—I'm relaxing, I'm letting go of the mother inside of me. I can't take my eyes off the photos of my sons. Max and Andrew look so beautiful to me, innocent still. I enjoy looking at their wonderful sweet faces for the first time in ages. Why? I'm determined to avoid passing on that part of my mother's heritage: the suspicion, the anxiety, the fear of weakness and exposure. I wish that I could sit next to Max and touch him kindly in some way. Curiously, I've never loved my mother more. I know she feels enormous love for me. I realize that her demands of me—the demands I could never satisfactorily meet—were reflections of her own insecurities. She, too, is a victim of her past.

I feel very relaxed. I feel free of the burden of my dear mother's expectations of me. The self remains to be discovered, but that feels a whole lot easier now. I'd love to make love to David right now, to be free to love him totally and wholly share with him. But of course, my roadblocks are only half the story—there remain his. I feel the absence of my manic laugh, my usual wiredness, an absence of resistance.

Seven P.M.

At dinner, for the first time I spoke with Rosslyn. To all appearances she's a very repressed Southern belle. Her grooming is impeccable, her manners exquisite. And in the dining room, over lasagna, she confided that she had twelve electroshock treatments here. I had no idea that this progressive place administers electroshock and I had no idea that someone as calm and polite as Rosslyn would be the recipient of the treatment. Good Lord, just when I think that I've got this place licked. Rosslyn talked about being certain that she'd been here three weeks—but her husband insisted it'd been five. She quietly and demurely described not wanting to live any longer when she arrived here. She had asked her husband, a minister, "Please take my life." She will turn thirty next week and has children eleven and six.

This evening I was sitting alone in the central lounge writing when Beth threw herself into my arms. "I am grieving," she sobbed. "There's been so much loss and I haven't had time to grieve. I've lost so much, I don't even have a bed. It's not fair, I'm so alone, I don't want to grieve alone." And she clung to me and sobbed her heart out and was ultimately pried away by a therapist.

I said, "No, Beth, it's not fair at all. Your loss is enormous and it's not fair." She asked, "Inette, will I make it? I'm so scared—will I make it?" And I said, "Beth, this is the bottom. You *will* make it because you run circles around most of the people out there, because I know something about you and there is so much there—you will make it." And she clung and she sobbed until we were pried apart.

I do know those feelings. Will I feel them again or am I already better for the almost two weeks here? Oh, Beth, I know each and every one of those damn feelings. I'm at the height of my meager powers now, so I can give what Connie and Kathy gave me only a week or so ago. I sit in the central lounge available to people, wanting to be available after Wylie. What a wondrous place.

The teenagers noisily bustle back from the gym as I write. Their noise and bustle, their endless energy, their electricity, the very charge of them—I don't know why they ever scared me; they seem so innocent, actually; full of electricity but still very much sweet children.

One A.M.

I just played a terrifically fun game of Trivial Pursuit and lost. The patients requested the game at the last Community Meeting and, *voila!* it appeared. Connie, Kathy, Coco, Kelly, Gary, and I played. We closed the lounge door to avoid having our hoots and laughter awaken the geriatric patients (who go to bed early). A nurse insisted we leave the door open. "They want the door open because the nurses are afraid we'll slit our wrists on the Trivial Pursuit pieces," I said. And then we all laughed because Kelly, a lovely, twenty-year-old junior enrolled at an elite Southern women's college, sat to my left with gauze-bandaged wrists. And Gary, a very handsome, bright, but quiet thirty-year-old sat to my right with identical bandages. Kelly and Gary laughed the hardest.

I also spent the night munching chocolate cookies. Beth has a theory that holds that chocolate contains the same chemical that is released by the female orgasm. She bolsters her case by arguing that during the sexy days before your menstrual period, you crave chocolate. So, while I devour all the chocolate I can get my hands on with no period in sight, the women of the lounge are taking great pleasure in describing my supposed horniness. In some ways, this lounge is a locker room.

Saturday, May 31

Charles Berman and I talked about David at length for the first time since I arrived. How will I handle him when I get out of here? (For the first time, I'm actually thinking of getting out.) As always, Charles reflects my own oft-repeated words and feelings back to me. My choices, he said, repeating the idea I've held tenaciously since David first left, are: "Go for it, give that relationship your all," or (Berman's alternative), "Write him your conditions and make them stick." Of course, I knew Berman's preferance but he skillfully avoided backing me into defensive corners. This time, I immediately answered, "I've *already* given that relationship my all, now I must set my conditions." Berman argues that David does love me, does want me, but also wants the kids and the wife if I permit that. Clearly I cannot. "There are all sorts of circumstances that prevent you and David from making it at this moment," he said. "Divorce is a process and none of this happens overnight."

Sunday, June 1

A new month, a new week—it feels promising. I awakened trying to compose whatever it is I want to say to David when I get home. In my inimitable way, I wrote a letter that rambled on for fifteen pages. Charles Berman acted as editor. "Short and sweet," he said. "A fifteen-page letter is *not* the way to tell someone you do not want a relationship—a fifteen-page letter *is* a relationship."

Today I went out on a pass with Paul and our sons. Most of the day was low-key, low-demand—sort of familylike. We sat in a park listening to live music. But around five o'clock, fireworks exploded that lasted for hours. I asked Paul whether he would bring the boys next Saturday or if he'd prefer Sunday. He hemmed and hawed and confessed he had plans to spend the weekend with another woman—and my children. I went crazy. I know we haven't lived together for five months, I know that I am in love with another man—yet still I'm capable of being threatened by the idea of another woman with my sons. For hours we fought. I said the ugliest things I could imagine—about him, about her. He called me a bitch, slamming his hamburger into the table at McDonald's. It was a white-trash public scene. Poor Andy was crying hysterically throughout. Paul said that he was unable to bring my kids to me two out of the three weekends I've been hospitalized because of "scheduling problems." Obviously there's something more like revenge going on here.

For six months I've shown no anger toward Paul because I've felt so damn guilty about David. I've never considered responding to Paul's anger with anger. But I'm no longer feeling guilty— I'm feeling mad. The score is even, I hate him, and I feel righteous anger.

Monday, June 2

This was my worst night since that first Tuesday. I was up most of the night, thinking about Paul and walking circles around these semidark hospital hallways. In the middle of the night there were these inhuman shrieks, animal-like, terrifying screams that continued for a half-hour and sent nurses racing through the corridors toward Unit Four and the new admission. I propped myself against the hallway wall, trying to read, and was told that I could not. I attempted middle-of-the-night phone calls to Paul and Charles Berman but was stopped in my tracks. It felt like a mental hospital last night: repressive, weird, frightening. It coincided with my own out-of-control jealousies about Paul. I'm so very unhappy. I feel so weak. Damn, damn Paul. I believe I want out of this marriage, but I do still care for him and probably always will.

Noon

Group therapy today took on the issue of my unreasonable jealousy. "You're jealous," Dr. Cannon said, "because you feel inadequate and you project that Paul is with the other woman because you *are* inadequate, not because you've rejected him." I feel this despite the fact that I know he still wants me. Further explanations of my anger and behavior yesterday: "You have the habit of anger whenever you feel vulnerable and inadequate," Dr. Cannon said. There's this separation in me of my intellectual life (my career and verbal abilities) and my emotional life. I don't allow the intellectual accomplishments to be part of my self-image—I still feel wanting emotionally. My intellectual defenses don't help me through my feelings of inadequacy.

Berman confronted me about Paul. "You're jealous because it's hard to see someone you care about with another woman," he said. "You're jealous because you do still care about Paul and he obviously adores you." Unless I'm willing to guarantee Paul a future, guarantee that I will not leave him again, said Berman, then Paul goes his way and I go mine—dealing only about the children. This was a rather impassioned session. Berman is good.

"You have a lot invested in competence," Susan Lewis said after Psychodrama today. "You have to let people know you need hugs. It's not as good when you have to ask."

Why is it that the more I learn about myself in these various therapies, the more confused I get? When a couple of things were first revealed, I felt on track, moving toward a destination. Now all tracks go in different directions. Each is just a beginning, nothing concludes.

Tuesday, June 3

I finally did my own psychodrama and it was an enormous disappointment. I'd been expecting so much of it. I could not let go of my guilt and I could not let go of my anger. In Terry's psychodrama, I was able to give vent to her rage, but in my own I was too controlled. Obviously it's easier for me to express my feelings through Terry than to deal with them directly. I'm confused and disappointed.

There was one scene we acted out—replaying my flying home from Boston with David last December, dreading telling Paul about the affair. Director Susan Lewis asked me what I felt at that moment, and I answered, "Like driving a motorcycle into a brick wall." I straddled a chair/motorcycle and the brick wall of patients moved inexorably toward me and I *was* petrified. At impact I was knocked with horrible force to the floor and the wall pressed painfully down on me, and Susan screamed, "Inette—let it go! Let it go!" At impact, I was to collapse in screams and tears, let go of the anguish and guilt—but I could not.

There was another scene from my early childhood that involved my next older brother forcing me to tackle and beat up some little girl I didn't even know. I refused to do it, but he bullied and threatened and taunted me until I did beat up that girl and I hated myself for it. In my psychodrama I reversed roles. I acknowledged my anger at my brother, tackled *him* to the ground, and beat him to a bloody pulp. In the midst of this revenge on my brother, Susan Lewis substituted Paul for my brother and I gasped with recognition of the anger I feel toward the man I married. But in the jargon of Psychodrama, "I couldn't complete."

There was a final scene that involved Paul, Max, Andrew, and me eating dinner at the farmhouse. Repeatedly the phone rang and summoned me away from the table—it was always David. There, off to the side, was David with his children tugging on each arm. Over and over I ricocheted—my family summoned me to the dinner table, David Muller called me to his side. And each time I made the same decision—I could not refuse to answer the phone, I could not refuse to go to David.

At the end of Psychodrama, Susan asked me, "Do you think marriage is forever and ever?" I answered, "Absolutely."

Seven P.M.

Beth and Terry suggested this morning that I consider moving to this city. It's an interesting idea that I can't let go of. I would be near my shrink, of course; Paul wouldn't be far from his kids; there would be new faces to meet and a lot more opportunity than in Watertown. It would be a genuine new beginning. It keeps rolling around in my head.

Today's therapies and insights: Charles Berman told me I'm leaving next Wednesday at eleven in the morning. Yikes! He just said it. I have a week to get used to the idea, to "process out" of this place, to let go, to pull the pieces together. Am I ready?

Biofeedback with Dr. Pedrozo. We mostly talked. "Be open," he said. "Open yourself to all sort of things, not just the tunnels that lead to Paul and David." And, "You will still have the exact same feelings when you get out of here. What you must change is the way you *think* about those feelings. Your feelings are your allies; you mustn't bury them." And, "Your mistake with David was going too fast. All of this takes time. You have a brilliant mind and a good hold on reality. Where you're flawed is in allowing the emotions to overtake you." Finally, he asked me, "Is the fear of being alone worth your life?" Of course, I now know, that it is not.

Wylie's Assertiveness group—"No one can make another person feel guilty. That's something you do to yourself. Neurotic guilt is the most useless of human emotions. You have remorse for something you legitimately regret, but neurotic guilt is useless."

Good friend Anna Farley phoned. She knows Paul and me well. "I know why you left Paul," she said for the first time. "You were his mother. He's very dear, but he never grew up."

Patient Beth asked me if David wasn't just a way to extricate myself from Paul and the marriage.

I believe that I'm now processing out.

Wednesday, June 4

This was a very strange night. An old lady from an Appalachian backwoods hollow was put in my room. At eleven P.M. she demanded to know, "You going to sleep already?" "Yes," said I. "You're going to be up all night," she prophesied. I fell promptly to sleep. At 3:30 A.M., when I was dead asleep, I heard a voice saying to me, "You're not sleeping, you're just faking. You're pretending to be asleep." I said, "God, what time is it?" She said, "Seven." I said, "No, it can't be, it's still dark." She said, "They'll tell you its three, but it's really seven." So I was awake with my roommate from 3:30 until she dressed and left at 5:30, and then I promptly fell back to sleep. She returned at 6:15 and demanded, "Are you going to sleep your life away?" "Only until seven," I pleaded. So finally—after two and a half weeks here—I will volunteer to relinquish my sunny room in the geriatric unit and my attempts at isolation. I have asked to be moved to the adult unit, but right now the lodge is full (Is the moon full?), so I can't be moved.

Four P.M.

Group therapy this morning yielded a genuine breakthrough. It was my first out-loud admission that my marriage is flawed. It was the first time I publicly admitted that my marriage does not fulfill my needs. I sat in the circle of six people and cried as I described Paul's wonderful qualities: "He's original, bright, a witty conversationalist, a great dancer, funny, kind, gentle, sensitive, a great father, and he loves me. Isn't that enough?!" And six heads shook, in unison, no. "No, Inette," one spoke for all, "that's *not* enough for you."

Dr. Cannon described my belief that Paul is the best I can do, all that I deserve. And David—who I describe as handsome, smart, accomplished, and high-powered—amazes me by actually loving *me*.

I've held so tenaciously to the idea that I had the "perfect marriage," even while I lived with another man, even until now. In fact, the fiction is my mother's idea about *her* marriage—not mine. It was her belief in the perfect marriage that I've held on to; it was her idea that all marriages last forever, but no longer mine. I am letting go.

The group talked about my need to be "respectable," to be approved of by everyone. "Your plan for the affair," Dr. Cannon said, "was that it be 'professional,' a fling completely apart from your marriage." That is true. I began the affair with the assumption that it would not and could not imperil my marriage. Dr. Cannon added, "You and Paul aren't as opposite as you see it. You both have dependency needs; you meet his, but he doesn't meet yours."

My marriage may actually be over. It seems to be over no matter what the story is with David, and I can barely stand the thought. How can I let go? I cry as I write this outside on a grounds' pass.

Thursday, June 5
I had the requisite family counseling with Paul. He looked particularly unattractive—dressed horribly, very overweight. It appeared to me that I had the home-field advantage. He was nervous, tense, unhappy, and not particularly clever. I was neither impressed nor attracted. Paul keeps repeating the same angry attacks he's directed at me for six months, but for the first time

I didn't respond with guilt. I didn't let my guilt blind me to my other legitimate needs.

Paul insisted on crediting me with "making me what I am," and I cringed when he said that. A good case can be made that he would never have gone to graduate school but for my ambitions for him and never completed it but for my insistence. In fact, every vacation Paul and I have taken was conceived, prodded, planned by me. Every move to each new city was my idea. Every garment Paul put on his body was of my choosing or with my approval. Every dinner party, every bit of décor was mine. All moves, save one, were for my needs or my career. And I have continually credited Paul with being exceptionally supportive of my work and needs—exceedingly unthreatened by a strong-willed wife. I thought the burden of our marriage was *his* to carry. That is what I've thought up until Hillsdale. Now I look at it differently: It was all up to me—if I didn't do it, it didn't get done, from the mundane to the sublime. Paul hated to make phone calls, just hated the phone, while I worked the phone like others work a chisel (it was a tool of my trade). That meant I called plumbers, babysitters, garages, and friends. Paul hated to deal with auto mechanics, salesmen, bankers, insurance people—so I did that, too. Paul had no manual dexterity, and though I was untrained, I loved the feeling of competence that came from building things from scratch or climbing under a sink to fix a leak—I did that, too. Granted, in these last years, Paul earned the salary and I cared for the children—but that disguised the many years I outearned him and it disguised the things that wouldn't function in our family if I didn't do them. He knew I would do the things he wouldn't; I knew I could do the things he couldn't.

After this week's team meeting, Charles Berman relayed my collective therapists' words. "You have done good work, you are ready to leave. No one is going to push you toward the marriage. Married or not, you and Paul will be good parents. No one but you can make the decision to end the marriage. You'll want a

relationship down the road that is more mutual—you've felt
sucked dry by yours, by everyone leaning on you. The new, more
mutual relationship down the road could be David and you, a
changed Paul and you, or some other. The team's advice is to
back off from both relationships now and go it alone."

I look forward to this summer with my children. I *will* mother
better when I get home. I want to enjoy them; to let them into
my life as a positive, comforting force—not always to view them
as burdens, trouble, or distraction from the more important me.
Watch out, summer, here I come! My sons and I will savor this
summer of their babyness and youth. God, I hope I find the
strength to do this well.

Six P.M.

I've officially moved into the adult unit, into Frances Ellen's
room. I've always thought of Frances Ellen as a wimp. It turns
out, oddly enough, that she's coming out of a two-year affair
with a married man. During the past two years, three wedding
dates had been set then broken by her lover. There were wonderful times and feelings—always followed by terribly destructive
ones. "I hope I never love you enough to leave my children,"
this man finally told Frances Ellen. Ultimately, as a result of this
relationship, my roommate became drug dependent, utterly self-
loathing, and suicidal.

She arrived here the day I did. I've seen the physical changes
in her as she grows stronger. She arrived disheveled and devastated. Lately, she's wearing makeup again, curling her hair,
and dressing up to go out on a pass.

Today she lectured me. She said, "As hard as it is to walk
away from David, you must set your conditions and make them
stick—you absolutely must. Otherwise, you will wind up hating
yourself. I would have been a lot better off if I'd drawn the line
one year ago." Still, this man visits her here; still she's in great
pain.

When I listen to Frances Ellen tell of her two-year affair or
to Kathy tell of her ten-year relationship, I'm strengthened. I

realize there will never be an easy time—a right time—to end it with David. I cannot trust David now; he doesn't know what he wants. He can only hurt me if I allow it. I can't allow it. I must not see him while he sits comfortably in his home. I cannot. But damn, it will be hard.

9:30 P.M.

I just got back from Connie's farewell dinner. Kathy, Gary, Connie, and I got passes and went on an outing in my car to a place called South Sea Island, a Polynesian restaurant with leis, of all things. It was an hilarious evening: lots of smut and lots of psych hospital humor, lots of crazy people jokes. Then we went to Baskin Robbins for hot fudge sundaes. This was a warm summer night, with the best of fellowship. Connie's leaving tomorrow is hard on all of us. It leaves a really big hole that won't be filled; the chemistry can't be duplicated and there are a lot of sad feelings. But tonight was the best of times—better than in a long time. Perhaps I can do just fine without David or Paul. Perhaps there can be fine times with new friends. Perhaps there is someone who will value me more than either of them have. Perhaps.

More and more, I'm thinking of moving here to Asheville. I like the distance (two hours) from Paul *and* David. The kids will do well here, I think. Tomorrow I'll go out with a realtor to study the neighborhoods of this town. It'll be terrific fun out there by myself, looking at the neighborhoods and deciding where *I* would fit, where the kids and I would fit—not Paul, not David. Just grown-up Inette doing the most grown-up of things—choosing where I want to live.

Here is my final letter to David in its final form. I have no idea at what point I'll send it.

Dearest David,
As always there is much I can say, but this time I'm going to do it in a few words.

I love you, Dave. I continue to want to be loved by you. I do not love you any less.

What the hospitalization was about was working on loving me more, not bluffing and blustering but learning to face down my own feelings about myself and coming out stronger. And I believe that I have. Ironically, as I love me more, I've grown to love you more.

For you, for me, for any future possible us: the conditions aren't so very changed, but my absolute commitment to them has been reinforced. I cannot love you at the expense of my self-worth. I can love you only when loving you and being loved by you enhance my good feelings about me. I would wish the same for you.

What does that mean? It means we can have *no* relationship while you are in your home, no relationship at all (no phone calls or letters) unless you have filed for divorce and have at least a temporary separation. It means if you are in your own apartment, working at discovering yourself and "processing" the divorce, I would want very much to see you and work on us.

When I think of us, I think we failed only to acknowledge the difficulty of what we attempted and the length of time the process takes. We also failed to understand that it's essential to realize the old marriage is unworkable before a new one can be forged. It does take time.

Again, there are no easy days ahead. But I can be responsible only for my own days. I can no longer put your or Paul's interests and feelings before my own. This is a letter, dear, dear David, that requires and desires no response from you.

> With deep and continuing love,
> Inette

Friday, June 6

Connie has left and I'm contemplative in my room after a grounds pass with Kathy and Kelly (Connie conspicuously absent). I'm a little melancholy—make that a lot melancholy—wanting only to spend the evening reading and writing.

I got a letter today from Amy, one of my few Watertown friends who are still friends. She wrote, "I have no idea what awaits you here upon your return, but Inette, your strength as a woman, an individual, are so obvious that I know you can handle it when the time is right." Thank you, Amy.

In recent days several people have referred to my strength. Kathy said, "I know you'll survive the trauma and come out stronger than ever—you've got the 'right stuff.' " Roommate Frances Ellen said, "You're so strong, you have so much character and energy." Beth asked if I can imagine another man in my life, and I said, "Sure." She answered, "I can imagine that for you, but I can't imagine that for me." I begin to believe in my own future—mine, defined by no one but me and my responsibilities for my two boys. I hope that this isn't false bravado that will dissipate at the sound of David Muller's voice. His voice— I can't remember it.

Wylie said in Cognitive, "The past is fantasy, the future is fantasy, only the present exists. Live in the present."

Sunday, June 8

Terry left this morning. Her husband, Alan, came and declared, "Let's get out of this place." I said, "These husbands come, claim their wives, and cart them off." And Kathy belted out the song, "Wedding bells are breaking up that old gang of mine." I laughed—it feels like that.

Familiar faces are thinning out, and I'm eating meals with unlikely people. Kathy is an island in the sea. We both think and wonder aloud about Connie. New people come in now and new clusters form. I'm on my way out, that much is clear.

Beth and I went out on pass for a Mexican dinner. Thoughts from Beth: "The clue I had about your marriage, Inette, was that you always said, 'My marriage'; you never said, 'Our marriage,' " And on David: "Let me put it this way, Inette, despite the fact that he's very handsome, despite the fact that he plays the piano well and reads poetry, despite the fact that he drives a Jaguar and gives you brass cappuccino machines, despite all of that—

I don't envy you at all. He wants you *and* the marriage, and that says something about how he views you. The woman on the back burner is the one who usually gets burned." Beth is complex, insightful, and very, very troubled. She and I may do each other some good. It was her shrink who said, "One month in Hillsdale equals one year of therapy."

Monday, June 9

My last group therapy. Dr. Cannon summarized. "Your greatest defense is perfectionism—that, and denial. You deny that anything is not perfect. You are terrified that when people see you in the light of day they will view you as imperfect." I have, of course, denied that my marriage was anything but perfect until last week—and then I felt great relief. Then, when Paul yelled at me in family counseling, I no longer felt guilty—I realized for the first time that we both created this imperfect marriage. "Your torrid affair," Dr. Cannon said, "was your way of acting out all your bad feelings toward the marriage—all your anger for what it didn't give you—and still not admitting it wasn't perfect." She admitted that she operates much the same way, and as I look and listen to her, I believe that she does. "Of course," she added, "no marriage, *nothing* is ever perfect, or can be."

"You appear so assertive," Dr. Cannon said, "but you're not. That's part of your sophisticated defense." *Here*—at last—I've allowed myself to be vulnerable, to acknowledge the scared little girl and the sensitive woman inside of me. Here I've come to realize that, like so many women, I've been the perpetual nurturer—loving a man unconditionally, sacrificing my needs for that man—in the vain hope that he'll come to love himself (and me). Now I face the decision about my marriage and Dr. Cannon said, "You can never be sure, never. You just have to accept that, too, and get on with it."

Tuesday, June 10

Tomorrow I go home. Dr. Berman gave me the chance to back out. "No," I said. "I'm ready."

Good-bye to Dr. Joe Wylie. "You know how I feel about you," he said. "And *you* know how I feel about you," I responded. "Yes, I do," he said. "It's stimulating to be around you, but I worried you might not see anything as *your* problem, as bright as you are—but you have, you have examined yourself." Berman asked me if there was any man here who I was attracted to, and he was fishing for the name of a certain patient. "Yes," I told him. "I'm definitely attracted to one man and it's Joe Wylie." So good-bye to my Dr. Wylie fantasies—not too far from a certain reality, under other circumstances. Good-bye to that.

Good-bye to Dr. Pedrozo, to his biofeedback machine and his stories about the other physician who took a full year in therapy to extricate himself from his twenty-year marriage and marry the woman he loved.

A last hug and good-bye from my primary therapist. She said, "I'm pleased with how you're handling this. If you carry all the guilt and blame, you'll end up back here." I don't want that to happen.

Good-bye after Aerobics to the physical-education therapist, who oversaw my last good workout to the album from *The Big Chill*. Another hug and more good wishes. This feels like graduation.

6:30 P.M.

I did it. In the second family counseling session, I told Paul I wanted out. In no uncertain terms, I said, "I want a divorce." He was in great pain—he was twice struck by lightning. "First you left me because you said you loved another man—and now you're telling me you just don't want me," he said through tears. "Tell me why," he demanded. "Because," I said, "I'm being sucked dry by our marriage, by your demands on me, by your needs, by the fact that I live both our lives." He responded: "I don't hear a reason. You're throwing out the baby with the bath water. What about commitment? What about all the years we've shared? You're being vague." I asked the family counselor, Jane, if this was true. She said to Paul, "You're not ready to hear this yet."

Paul sat there suffering and all my instincts were to take him in my arms and comfort him, to ease his pain as I've always done. But I appreciated the irony of protecting him from the pain that I was inflicting. I held my arms tightly at my sides.

"You've never said that you're sorry for the pain you caused me—never," he accused. So I told him, "Paul, I'm so very sorry for the unconscionable pain that I'm inflicting on you." And then he bolted out of that place, tears on his cheeks, fear in his eyes—and I was flooded again with guilt.

Bless her heart, an hour after the session, Kathy intervened. "Repeat, Inette, *'Remorse, not guilt.'* " She told me that I needed a man I respected, and right now it appeared that I didn't respect Paul. I cried, we walked the grounds, and she said all the right things. Now I'm again free of the guilt. In fact, I feel some sense of relief—I've finally, straightforwardly said it, "I want out of this marriage because it's no good for me."

Wednesday, June 11

D-Day and I'm ready. I slept well, I ate well. I'm excited and calm and happy. I'm ready to take on what the world throws at me. I'm certain it will be a truckload. I love this place. I love it for what it has done for me. And because what this place does is make you ready to leave it, I'm ready to leave.

Dr. Berman and I exchanged our last good-bye here. I'll see him in his office, as an outpatient, on Monday. He said, "You did the kindest thing you could do for Paul at this point." The family counselor said, "You did a brave and courageous thing."

Kathy, Kelly, and Gary signed out for grounds passes and walked me to my car. Kelly's words were the last. "Inette, you're history."

My chest is full to bursting as I drive the slow mountain roads to Watertown and I am afraid.

Part VI

BETWEEN PLACES

Wednesday, June 11

I'm here at home in Watertown, having leaped that huge chasm from *there* to here, from sheltered to exposed, from social to alone, from safe to vulnerable. The phone rang once and it was for Dr. Muller—obviously physician recruiters. I needed to look up his home number in the phone book to tell these people where they might find him. In the Kroger's checkout line, a colleague of David's stood wordlessly behind me. Every single thing here is colored, Asheville is where I *must* be. This place will be too hard for me. Nevertheless, I am here for now, and I will deal in my best way. Charles Berman's last words reverberate, "Things will definitely get better—remember, they will get better."

I keep looking for ironic symbolism in this plague of the seventeen-year locusts that is upon us. Ugly, humming, huge, nose-diving, leaf-eating bugs are everywhere. I vividly remember being a child on Woodbrook Avenue in Baltimore and being terrorized by these disgusting locusts—perhaps I was six.

Thursday, June 12

This was a very, very lovely day with my sons. Together today, we played cards, rode bikes, watched planes take off at the airport, decorated Father's Day cards, took a long walk, cooked and ate their favorite french toast breakfast and pasta dinner. I enjoyed every moment with the boys. They rewarded me for my attention by going to bed without complaint, and immediately to sleep. The children are central now, very central. After almost four weeks away and months of a raging and distracting love affair, nothing else can matter as much.

Max messed his pants three times today. The last time, I yelled in exasperation, and he poignantly asked, "Mom, are you mad at me?" Then he told me, "I'm a mean boy." Later he said, "I will marry you—you won't need David." I did my best to address these issues but mostly I just lavished complete attention on each child. And because I'm calm and relaxed, they are. Lord, it's true, if I'm happy, I treat them well and they are happy—it's that simple. They've had a lot of the inverse of that lately.

I think about the hospital, so far away—very far away. I am glad to be home (I wasn't sure that I would be). But I think of Kathy and Beth and Frances Ellen, and Gary—and, of course, Dr. Wylie—in the lounge now. Life goes on there, but I am gratefully here.

Saturday, June 14

Yesterday's mail brought a very destructive letter from my former close friend Ellen. She left her husband for another man a few years ago, but never forgave me for doing the same thing. After six months of the cold shoulder, she greeted my return from a psychiatric hospital with these words.

I felt that any communication would be interpreted by you as a form of approval and acceptance. . . . I was very troubled by the cruelty of your behavior. . . . It was a gross act of self-delusion and self-indulgence. . . . I felt you were cruelly irre-

sponsible and reckless in your abandonment of your marriage—
of Paul, of the children, in a sense. . . . You've done what many
people have done—been a fool in this life—fucked up
big. . . . Inette, you messed up in a big way. Admit it, learn
from it. Find a little humility and compassion and selflessness in
that miserly heart—maybe a bit less arrogance. . . .

It felt like Ellen—this woman who had been a friend—had
kicked me in the belly. And all the while, she was feeling virtu-
ous for "reaching out." I sat stunned and alone in the apartment, mulling over possible responses, and the phone rang. It was
Kathy calling from the hospital to check me out. "This is not a
friend," she said. "Do not answer the letter—any answer will
seem defensive. Throw it in the trash can." Thank God for
that call.

Another older and wiser friend offered an assessment of my
situation today. Martin Farley—Anna's husband—is a well-known
academic and, to some degree Paul's mentor, but a friend to each
of us. "You come out emotionally the worst in this triangle,
Inette," he said. "Paul has the support and solace of friends,
David has his practice and his kids—but you are twice rejected
by the man you love."

Is it possible that David doesn't know I'm here? I drove past
his office yesterday. I find excuses to drive past his office just to
look at his Jeep in the parking lot.

My dearest and oldest friend, Ronnie, called from Cleveland.
I love her heart. She's coming for a visit. She and Ed, the couple
most completely like Paul and me in dynamics and personality,
are "having problems." She couldn't talk on the phone, it will
have to await her visit. I don't want to feel a sense of relief that
their lives are falling apart, too—the lives of the couple closest
to us. What sort of pervert am I? But I need to see her, I do.
Ronnie first called Hillsdale to find me and was told, "I'm sorry,
she's no longer here." "Well, I'm not," retorted Ronnie, "I'm
glad."

Sunday, June 15

Father's Day. Damn, damn, damn! What does Muller *do* this Father's Day? I leave my front door open so he'll know I'm here if he drives past. I'm clearly obsessing about this man. I want him to call so I'll have an excuse to mail my psych hospital letter. How do I tell him we can have no relationship at all, if he doesn't ask for one? I'm at loose ends, I better gather myself up. I have the Asheville paper here and I should be answering apartment ads—but I'm feeling shaky.

Damn it all—it's time to give myself a pep talk. Asheville, here I come! I *will* rebuild my life. I *will* take risks. I *will* relearn what it feels like to be alone. I *will* take care of my boys. And as my friend from New York City said by phone, "If David finds he's able to free himself—it won't be so easy for him this time around—you'll be rebuilding your life."

Monday, June 16

I'm exhausted from a long day in the Asheville heat. I spent the bulk of the day scouring the neighborhood I've chosen (old, tree-lined, architecturally eclectic, and upper crust) for a home— but I had no luck. There are few rentals in that neighborhood that conform to my needs—a yard for the kids and three bedrooms—and those that do are exceedingly expensive. This neighborhood is attractively privy to the best public elementary school in the city. I'll keep looking, but it seems that it may take time— time that I must live in claustrophobic proximity to David in Watertown.

I had a session with Charles Berman today. He approves of my satisfaction with and pleasure in the children—he wants to encourage *that* direction. He knows I've been waiting for a call from David that hasn't come. "Talking to David would be a simultaneous low and high," he warned. "I fear you'll lose the ground you've gained this month, if you speak to him now. I'd like to see more distance between you and David." He accused me of wanting to mail my letter to engage David, not to sever him. He said the letter is no longer necessary. So are David and

I over? Will he reappear in a year, in five years? Berman asked me to describe the man I'd like to meet and marry some day. I can't imagine loving a man who is neither Paul nor David.

I have no control over David, no meaningful control. I can draw him to me in inconsequential ways but not over the long run. *He* has to reject that marriage to choose me. He has to do with Linda what I do with Paul. And he cannot now—maybe he never can. So what does he have to give me? Very, very little. I must put him behind me.

This month's *Cosmo* has a story titled "The Worst Thing Anyone Ever Said to Me." I have no problem selecting mine. It was May 18, that last night David and I were together. After promising me the moon, describing in some detail the glories of our future—our married future—he returned from his home and the scene with his children and told me that his earlier words were "Hemingway bullshit." God, it hurts to remember that.

Tuesday, June 17

I'm looking in the mirror and really liking what I see today. David Muller was right—I am a good-looking woman, full of herself, full of life, smart as hell. On the phone the other day, my mother told me that "beauty is on the inside," thereby affirming that I have no beauty on the outside. But this time I laughed. Her messages are clear, but I no longer buy them.

The boys are bathed, fed, entertained, and in bed. I'm still feeling like a good and competent mother. I've shown patience and I've kept Max and Andy as my prime focus.

But I'm specifically premenstrual tonight—which means that, at best, I'm subject to free-floating anxieties and, at worst, I'm headed for heavy depression. This time last month, I was walking alone on a grounds' pass and was struck by the realization that Paul and David had talked—and I freaked out. But tonight, when I found myself saying that David and I are verily over— that this is all she wrote—I still managed to play Go Fish with Max, still made the boys a decent dinner, and still believed that I look and am okay. That has to pass for progress. I know there are tough times ahead, but I also know that I'll do better than survive.

I *am* doing better than just hanging on. The future is the future; it cannot be known. But today I do know and I am managing. I push off of my marriage via David into new growth and challenge and David settles back—without contentment, assuredly—but with some sense of having done the right thing. The first month that David was gone, I wrote letters to him incessantly. Now in our third month apart, I'm writing solely for me, and that too is progress.

I think about all I face in a move to Asheville: the dislocation, the loneliness, the expense. On the surface and in the lists I write and rewrite, it looks cheaper and easier to stay in Watertown—I already have a home I like, a babysitter who's crazy about Andy, a good teaching job. So why, I ask myself, do I want to put myself through lots of stress and expense? And there are only two reasons. I have to get away from the shadow of David, and some distance from Paul wouldn't be such a bad idea, either.

I have two immediate goals. I must find a place to live in Asheville and I must get myself to New York City to find freelance writing work.

I do love keeping this journal. I'm convinced it'll tell quite a story of human need.

Wednesday, June 18

I've been out of the hospital for one week. It's been a month to the minute since David offered his last promise of a future— a promise he retracted several hours later. I fear that he believes I hate him, that he carries enormous guilt for having driven me to a mental hopsital—that he hates himself. I want him to know that I do not hate him—I do not hold him responsible for my decisions and choices.

I bumped into a woman who's been very kind to me throughout this trauma, who visited me often in this apartment last Winter. "I can't get over how calm you appear," she said. "This is the calmest you've been since you left Paul. Even when you said you were happy, you were not calm." That's absolutely true.

I hired a cleaning woman to scour the farmhouse in preparation for sale. She did and then told me it just sparkled. She went on about how terrific the kitchen looked (the kitchen I remodeled two months before I left) and how great the kids' bedrooms looked. I went to her house to pay her and I was dying to see the place shine, but I didn't trust myself emotionally to go there.

I had no luck on Asheville house rental calls. The last person rudely cut me off with, "We do not take children." I have to keep chugging.

Thursday, June 19

One month ago tonight, I entered Hillsdale Psychiatric Hospital. What a night that was. With very little effort, I can summon the emptiness, the fears, the senselessness, the hopelessness. One month. May 19 will always be one of those dates.

Today I called my old friend the magazine editor and elicited names of other editors and literary agents. I set the date for my week in New York City and booked a flight for July 13. I scoured the Asheville paper for rentals. Today I toted the red upholstered chair whose spring burst shortly before David left (he futilely attempted a quickie repair) to the repair shop. Now that feels like an accomplishment. That chair with the popped springs has been a constant accusation of my inability to cope. Today I had the boys and cared for them. Today I answered a phone call asking for Dr. David Muller with petulance and anger, but that was the worst of it. Today I think I will be able to make a life without Paul or David.

Friday, June 20

David is, of course, no longer the alternative to a marriage with Paul. But what David still is, is a reminder of an alternative style of relating: one that doesn't burden me with the care of my spouse; one that excites me with the equality. Hmmm. Were David and I equals? Did I give more than I should have? I really have not examined that relationship. Hillsdale was about examining me, of course, and my marriage to Paul. First things first.

Later in the day

It hasn't been a terrific day. I found three separate and different reasons for driving past David's office. It makes me crazy to do that. Then Paul called and talked about *his* feelings for a half-hour. "This is it, this is really it? You mean what you say?" he asked. Shit, now I have a hard time getting Paul out of my mind. Damn it all—get me out of here. Berman's partner's words echo: "For six months your life will be the pits, at nine months you'll be out of it, and in one year you'll be ready to form another relationship."

I just may hate David for the regularity of his old life. He steps right back in with only minor interruptions of his surgery and his Garden Club wives' parties. But I think, "How *can* he exist like that?" For me, at least, all is new—terribly, terribly hard, but new and not to be compared. For him it's the same old horror.

And, of course, there is sex. I lay in bed this morning specifically fantasizing the anatomical possibilities of sex with David— it has to be David. I am capable of anger at Muller, but that's stupid and beside the point. The point is me and how I handle *my* life. I cannot entice, provoke, enchant, tempt, convince, or reason with David Richard Muller again. It has to come from him. So Inette, lay off, get on with it—and get off Paul's case, too.

Saturday, June 21

Max just left for Baltimore. This is his first week alone with grandparents, though the invitation was issued a year ago. I'm excited for him.

I seem to be slipping—I feel like I'm losing ground, losing my hospital gains. It's a hot summer weekend when all good folks are sunning, swimming, or canoeing on the river and generally enjoying life. I, on the other hand, am some sort of purposeless anomaly. I'm already tired of making all my own plans all of the time, filling all of my own hours. Life is certainly going to get harder before it gets easier.

My parents called to tell me Max arrived safely. My mother asked how I was. "Ups and downs," I answered. She said, "I only want to hear about the ups." I said, "That's bluff and baloney—life *is* ups and downs." She was quiet, then conceded, "That's true." I felt I had scored the first point of my adulthood.

Monday, June 23

There's been a leap here, a remarkably spontaneous one for me. I'm in Hilton Head, South Carolina, in a very comfortable four-bedroom home. I'm looking out this window at a live oak tree dripping with Spanish moss. The Atlantic Ocean and beautiful stretches of white sandy beach are a half-mile away. How is it that I'm here?

Forty-eight hours ago, with Andrew in bed, I decided to treat myself to a long distance call to my sorely missed friend from Hillsdale, Connie Evans. It was then nine P.M. and she told me that, at midnight, she, Al, and the children were driving to Hilton Head, where a client of Al's had offered his sumptuous beach house, gratis. Al got on the phone and invited Andrew and me to come along. Connie loved the idea and insisted it would be wonderful if we joined them. *Of course,* I refused. First of all, I never accept politely offered hospitality that will inconvenience a friend, and second, I never act with that kind of spontaneity. Well, so much for *nevers.* "First off," Al persisted, "you are great fun—and second, we think you need it." "No, no, no, thank you," I demurred. "No, I've got to see the lawyer and a chair is being delivered and there are realtors in Asheville and I have lunch with a friend on Thursday—and I'd have to make a dozen calls." Connie answered, "Bullshit—just come. All that can be canceled, start packing, we'll meet you in two hours." And you know, I did. Andrew slept as I threw groceries and beach chairs and rafts and bathing suits and toys into the car. Hell, I decided, I am going.

Connie and Al make it all so easy for me. They demand so little. I pay for very little (just my gas, my suntan lotion—they won't accept grocery money). Their twelve-year-old daughter Rachel is a natural and affectionate babysitter for Andrew. In fact, all the Evanses are terrific to Andrew and he is glorying in his only-childness. He is his usual sweet self, and this becomes the best of all vacations. Plus—as my journal reflected—I was headed for a bad, bad state with regard to David and Watertown. I had to get out of there. The whole ride down I bitched at Connie about David and that damn small town. But today— ahh, today—I'm so glad I did this for me.

Wednesday, June 25

My life has been so easy that I have no inclination at all to be writing in this journal. Connie just wandered by and said, "Give me a break—take a vacation from that journal."

Last night Connie and I walked around Harbortown, a commercial waterfront development, licking good ice cream and talking lives and marriages. Her dilemma is trying to fix a marriage after an affair—the continued commitment to the marriage versus the continued rage and unfulfilled needs within the marriage. My dilemma lies in the pain of severing the old marriage—and the affair—and the fears of building a new life alone.

We walked past huge private boats, and I thought of David's recurrent dream of owning a boat and the hard time I gave him about it. Why? I love boats, why did I hassle him? I love nice things, why did I deny that? I love being treated well, why did I refuse him? My God, there's been a lot unresolved in the hurry, hurry of our relationship. I would *so* like a crack at a slower-paced, less encumbered love of him. Give it time, Inette.

I feel warm and cared for here. Connie sits and rubs my feet while I watch TV. She folds my laundry. She tells funny stories about my son. Al calls me "gutsy, strong" and says, "I'm sure things will work out for you." They're such good people.

Sunday, June 29

I'm back from Hilton Head and I'm exhausted from the drive. The moment, the very moment I arrived, my thoughts locked onto David.

I have my work cut out for me this week. I have to set up appointments with New York magazine editors and to talk to a book agent. I'm looking for a college teaching job in Asheville, and of course, there is still the search for a place to live. I need this week without children to get it all done, but I've come to depend on them, too. I bitched at Paul tonight when he picked up the boys because I hated handing over my sons to him—I was feeling very possessive.

I later called Paul to apologize for the way I behaved and we fought bitterly. "You called me because you feel shaky—Hillsdale isn't working for you anymore," he taunted. We called each other names. Obviously, I blew it by calling him. But I'm not off the deep end. I've just let off some steam and I guess we have to expect this. How civilized can two people be who are ending a sixteen-year marriage? The hospital still helps if I can say this to myself.

Monday, June 30

All morning, my anxiety focused on—of all things—health insurance. It appears that there is no way I can continue my sessions with Dr. Charles Berman after the divorce. I'm currently insured by Paul's employer, who by law must convert me to a policy of my own after the divorce. However, that employer will convert me only to a policy that doesn't include psychiatric coverage. Any new policy I get independently won't cover "preexisting conditions," and my shaky emotional state qualifies as a "preexisting condition." So I'm literally between the devil and the deep blue sea. I can't afford my expensive shrink without insurance: if I remain married I can continue to see Berman, but when I divorce, I'm effectively cut off from my therapy. Lord.

Interspersed this morning among my calls to the state insurance commissioner, my lawyer, and the personnel office of Paul's em-

ployer—all futile attempts to get insurance—were equally futile
stabs at finding a place to live in Asheville and a teaching job.
It was intensely humid and I thought I just might be on the brink
of a relapse. I was feeling anxious and full of tears and sure that
I could not make it—that I could not get writing jobs or go to
New York or do any of the stuff I need to do to support myself.
I was feeling frail, more fragile than I've felt since before the
hospital.

But in midafternoon, it turned around. I spoke to a few New
York magazine editors and—at length—to my friend's terrific
agent. All were quite receptive and welcoming, so I overcame
my intense fear of cracking that nut. There's still lots of work
to be done, but I'm back on track, and earlier today, I wouldn't
have dreamed that I could be. I may—please, God—be writing
again.

Paul—I'm feeling resentful of him these days. I fed him constantly—he demanded and I gave. But the irony is, we always
saw it the other way (that I demanded and he gave). Even now,
with all the trials I face, the addition of Paul is another burden,
not an easing of mine. I'm not inclined to give to him now, I'm
not inclined to be compromising. David and Linda are a lot like
Paul and me in reverse. He believes that *he* demands and she
gives, but in truth, it's the opposite. And it does wear you out.

Tuesday, July 1
I'm tired. This was another day spent attacking the New York
magazine world. I actively tried to convince editors that it was
to their distinct advantage to see me when I'm up there. Some
people were lovely and gracious in the outside-of-New-York-City
norm, while others were brusque, rude, and arrogant—the New
York City stereotype. I dealt with both—though the former, of
course, with greater ease. I'm feeling very gutsy, hard working,
healthy, and high on myself.

I rewrote my hospital letter to David, made it a bit longer. I
feel proud of each day, week, and month that passes without
sending it. But I know eventually I will.

It's later in the day and I'm getting ready for bed. I look at my body in panties and bra, and it looks a bit more abundant than I like but highly sexual. I moan, "David," and I rub my own belly and thighs. "Oh, David, it's been so long. What *does* it feel like to touch you, to have you make love to me?" My God, constant children do keep you from these thoughts and feelings. My God, the wonderful sex that is missing from my life and I've only just noticed. How does David handle his sexuality now? Perhaps it's a question I don't want answered. He's living with a woman, I'm not living with a man.

Thursday, July 3

I did it. I'm going to move to Asheville. I've agreed to rent a small house in the nicest neighborhood of the city. It's an uninspiring 1950s rambler, but it's adequate. The street is tree-lined; the house has three bedrooms, a good-size living room, a dining room, and a full attic. There are hardwood floors, hookups for my washer and dryer, and front and back tree-filled yards. It's four blocks from the best elementary school in the city. If Asheville works and the farm sells, in a year, I'll buy a house in this neighborhood.

From the moment I agreed to rent the house, I felt myself soaring into this new life. I'm busily making lists of things to be done in preparation for the move: school transcripts transferred, bank accounts opened and closed, telephones disconnected and reconnected, movers hired and moving dates set, utilites canceled, and many boxes to be packed. And I have to tell Paul!

Apart from the move—I must still call editors, generate story ideas, and resolve the issue of health insurance. Next week is wall-to-wall kids.

Look out, Asheville—here I come! How is it that someone with so little money has such high hopes, big plans, and the determination to take that town by storm? Being a big fish in that little pond sounds very comforting to me right now. And Asheville looks like an ocean compared to Watertown.

I had dinner with an older friend who is widowed and currently involved with a man who's separated from his wife, but definitely not divorced. It's funny, but when Rose talks about her Henry, I can easily spot where *that* relationship is not going. She's waiting for him to renounce his sick connection to his wife for the greater love of her. I can tell *her*, "Give him an ultimatum"; or, "He'll never free himself without therapy"; or, "Look out for yourself." I can think, "There's no way she isn't going to end up hurting." I can say and think these things about Rose, and still tonight, I sat with headlights off in a dark hospital parking lot waiting to pounce on a moment's conversation with David Muller.

Friday, July 4

My friend Wendy is back from a six-month massage school in Florida and offered me the gift of a free massage. I was driving to her home when I saw David's face for the first time since before the hospital. We passed each other on the road. His hair was cut short, and I strained to make him out through the opaque windshield of his Jeep. We waved like robots to each other—arms shot up, there were no smiles, and he was gone. Only the heavy emphatic pounding of my blood remained.

I continued to Wendy's. She massaged my neck, shoulders, and back for two hours. I hadn't seen her since last December, and as she massaged, I told her my story. The stroking freed my words. Wendy is perhaps one of my more intuitive and spiritual friends. She took one look at me and said, "Inette, you look deeper, deepened, older—but not as opposed to younger—more adult, less child. You look good, better."

When I drove home after the massage, an acute anxiety and desperation set in. The anxiety, the desperation, built in my chest for about an hour, and then it exploded. For one half-hour, there were gut-wrenching, chest-heaving cries. "I can't make it. Dave, Dave, Dave—I *need* you." These were heaving, face-contorting screams of pain. There were anguished pleas for David to end my loneliness, my horrible loneliness. This was fear, fear for my future—alone in that strange city. This was the first time in all these godawful days that I have cried so determinedly and endlessly without a soul to hear my cries. It was deep and prolonged and painful.

My anguish built, welled up, and spilled over into halting, deep sobs. And now it's over and I lay in my bed enervated. The oppressive buildup in my chest is gone. The terror, anxiety, hopelessness are gone. I'm over whatever that was. The first of its kind—or the worst of its kind—but my God, it's over.

Tonight, I mailed my letter to David. I cannot tolerate the thought that he doubts I love him—that after the hospital and whatever Paul conveyed to him, he thinks I hate him. I cannot hold back my love and increase his pain another minute. This letter, the psych hospital letter, is the *very last* communication. I hope I did the right thing. The letter is explicit in requiring no response, so I will never know if he got it, never know his reaction. There isn't one more thing for me to do, but await a bolt of lightning to hit David Richard Muller. When I get to Asheville, it'll be easier—just the proximity here is wearing me out.

Sunday, July 6

I'm feeling pessimistic—pessimistic that I'll make it as a writer, that I'll be happy in Asheville, that David will ever again tell me he loves me and wants me, that I'll ever again love a man or be loved by one the way I loved David.

My resolve is weakening. At times I feel I'd rather have any relationship with him than none. I'll be his lover—let him keep his wife, if I can just be with him. And why not? Because, I must convince myself, eventually he won't want that either and I'll progressively feel like shit. I tell myself that I know he loves me and yet he's able to choose his family. So it's parallel for me to say, I know I love him, but I must choose my self-esteem— and that means not seeing him.

Already before my letter has reached him, I fantasize an October 23 letter commemorating the anniversary of the beginning of the affair. I think that I will send him a duplicate of my original note. And then, in December, I fantasize a fortieth-birthday letter, "Happy birthday, another one without you. I hope your fortieth is as wonderful as mine." But of course, Charles Berman would never approve of my acting on these fantasies.

Monday, July 7

Today I was greeted by a good woman friend of David's with warm hugs. "David told me, 'They were the best six months of my life and I learned a lot from them.' " she said; "for what that's worth." I answered, "I know that, and it's not enough."

Tuesday, July 8

Another person tells me today that David looks like shit, that he's lost an unconscionable amount of weight and he looks drawn and haggard.

The New York ducks are lining up. All editors have agreed to see me. I've still got my story ideas to work up, but at least I've got my foot firmly in the door—ten meetings set up, not bad action.

Wednesday, July 9

I'm afraid of New York City, that high-pressure proving ground. I have to get work to justify the expense of the trip, the quickly dwindling money. I'm afraid of the pressures of New York City, the big leagues—of having to put myself on the line for rejection.

I'm afraid of Asheville, the new house, the loneliness, the kids without a sitter, so little money.

In Watertown, everyday I meet someone who has drawn conclusions about why David left me; and everyday I fight buying their interpretations of *my life*—with decreasing effectiveness. I don't know anymore what it is David feels or felt, I don't even know anymore what it is I feel or felt.

And still I have to deal with Paul to get my things out of that farmhouse. I dread that.

These are the things that keep me up most of the night. These are the things that obliterate any crack at tranquillity. My only immediate goal is getting to Friday's psychotherapy without calling Berman first. On days like these, it's hard to see that I'm improving in any way.

Am I wise to put myself under these external stresses and pressures? Do I have any choice at all? I do not. I cannot stay here. I must support myself. I must care for my children. I cannot live with Paul again. David cannot live with me. So, the stresses and pressures are inescapable. I must plug on. Shit, at least I am living. This is life—the pain, the fears, the hurts. I've opted to live. And my boys are doing well, I'm a more than adequate mother, it is summer.

Thursday, July 10

I just wrote forty change-of-address notes to friends and family. These are gracious, formal, little white cards announcing, "Inette Miller, Max, and Andrew invite you to visit, write, or call us at our new home after August 1 . . ."

This time, *this* move will be done with style. This time there'll be no skulking around in the night with crooked fingers pointing at me, no waiting for David to arrive, no waiting for David to pay the movers. This time, the move is wholly and completely mine—made with my money, my initative, my kids, my life, my little white note cards of announcement. Hurray.

Friday, July 11

I've spent hours rereading this journal from the beginning of the affair last October through January. I'm amazed and overwhelmed at the tremendous guilt I carried for Paul. Damn, I'm finally aware of what all those therapists dancing on the head of a pin call "the process" of divorce. The January guilts and fears are simply not here. I'm sure that Hillsdale was the pivotal phenomenon, but all of it, absolutely all of it—being with David and without, the ups and downs with the kids, the intense relations last winter with Paul—are all part and parcel of that process. There's no shortcut. I reread my own words, and now I believe Charles Berman's assurance that my life will be hard, but it will progressively get better.

Saturday, July 12

I'm in a very blue funk. I'm full of nerves and negativity. I'm full of yearning for what Charles Berman always calls my "great white father"—David Muller—to fill in my emptiness and self-doubt, to fill up my spaces.

Sunday, July 13

I'm in the Asheville airport on my way to New York City. Here are my thoughts. Maybe there could have been a more genteel and gentler way to escape my marriage than the one I chose. Did I choose? The reality is, there was no other way for me. As Paul said to someone months ago, "If Inette was going to have an affair, this is exactly the way Inette would do it—it's completely characteristic of her."

So, I sit here in the airport and fantasize—how would I defend my actions on the *Phil Donahue Show* or some other imagined public forum? Let's see:

"I was in love." (No, not in the beginning.)

"I was trapped, I was smothered by Paul."

"I was crazy."

"I was prodded by David." (Even *I* don't believe that.)

"There *is* such a thing as a midlife crisis."

"I have no excuse at all—it seemed right at the time."

I'd say, "It was right for me to get out of the place I was—I may have acted erratically, but I was acting in my best interest."

No, maybe I should say, "There's no defense. I'm not recommending the behavior. It isn't a philosophy or religion that I'm promoting. I'm simply recording the feelings and the story and I expect an awful lot of people may identify with them."

Would I do it again? I couldn't do otherwise.

Thursday, July 17

I've been in New York City since Sunday. I've seen eight top magazine editors, one twice, and my new book agent twice. I've charmed and been charmed. I've generated story ideas, regurgitated story ideas, restructured story ideas, sold story ideas—

sold me. This is the first two-hour stretch I've had all week
without a thing to do. I'm unusually exhausted, but my enthusiasm for each and every magazine, for each and every new editor
or publisher I meet, defies the exhaustion. I've been witty, sparkling, bright, and enthusiastic where appropriate. My agent says
of me, "You can't put a show horse in front of a plow." But
then, we all know that Inette does interviews well. Less certain
to me as I leave here, armed with work to be done, is—can I
deliver? Can I still write? Can I do what I say I do?

I have lots of work ahead to get this professional show on the
road, but I've done a hell of a job of laying the groundwork.
Still, there are the kids and their needs and the logistics of a
move to negotiate.

Wednesday, July 23

I have been home since yesterday, and there's no one to share
my New York stories with, no one to tell that I had breakfast at
the Algonquin Hotel.

I called my lawyer, Sherry, and she passed on the news that
David and Linda and family are going sailing in Greece next
month. And this has just blown my mind. We had planned (at
my suggestion) a sailing trip off Turkey this summer. So he rents
the boat in Greece instead of Turkey—he borrows on the theme
of Inette to make his marriage go. So he's working that hard to
make his marriage work. So I'm just out of a psychiatric hospital
and he is planning a trip to Greece. So—as Sherry says—"Some
people are just determined enough to stay together until the kids
are grown."

Shit, shit, shit. All the accomplishments of New York don't
add up to a pile of shit when I'm here. My walking around
Manhattan feeling attractive, classy, and bright—even in that
place—dissipates into tears now. I feel friendless and I want to
call my old friend Paul when I feel like this.

I called Paul and that's inexcusable. I called because I wanted
to talk to Paul about New York. Damn, I am weak. Sherry
listened to me describe my hustling after New York work and

she asked, "If you'd been doing this a few years ago, do you think
your marriage could have been saved? The thought just occurred
to me while you talked." She's not the first person to suggest
that.

Sunday, July 27

Al Evans, Connie's husband, called this afternoon. He poses
the other side of the picture—the side that tries to reconstruct
the marriage after the divorce. For that matter, it's David's side.
But Al is miserable; he can't allow himself to forgive or trust
Connie. He thinks they should separate for a while and she
responds with suicide threats. He sometimes thinks he stays only
because of her dependence. But I *know* there's more. I listen and
I talk as best I can. I want the Evanses to stay together and I
believe that they must and will. I don't wish the same for the
Mullers—I hope that David finds the courage to leave. Am I
deluding myself?

Paul and I are now legally separated, all the papers have been
signed. Divorce is being delayed until after January 1 because a
new federal law will then require Paul's employer to offer me
conversion insurance identical to what I have now. By waiting
until then, I can continue my therapy without interruption in
health insurance coverage. Paul has agreed.

Tuesday, July 29

I'm packing up this apartment and I'm having definite jabs of
anxiety. I realize—I am leaving David! I am leaving any chance
of acting a part in this drama, relinquishing an active role. And
it fucking scares the shit out of me. I want him! I want to talk
to him! I want to write, "Gone!" on his windshield. I don't want
to betray him by ever making love to another man.

I pack up the cappuccino machine he bought me. I find his
belt stuck in the back of a closet. I leave here, leave any trace
of the place we loved and shared. I leave the chance of passing
on the street. I leave the possibility that he drives past this
apartment in the dark of night. I pack up the teapot and the

toaster and the clock radio and the phone we bought to set up our household here together. Oh, my God, I hadn't thought it would be so devastating—this leaving. I anticipated the strangeness and loneliness of Asheville, but I hadn't thought of the quitting here until now—when it smashes me over the head as I box up my kitchen for the second time in seven months.

Oh, my God, closing out my life in this apartment may well be as hard as relinquishing Paul and the farm last January. David left me. Now I am leaving him.

Part VII
BEGINNING AGAIN

Friday, August 1

I expect and I hope that this is as bad as it gets. But, of course, I cannot know. I'm in the very same Dairy Queen in Cliff Top where I stopped to eat on my way to the Hillsdale Psychiatric Hospital—but now I'm leading a moving van over these mountains. Today's meal is identical to the one I had that other night, heavy on the fats and fried carbohydrates—not very healthy.

This morning I watched the contents of 100 Foster Street, Apartment 2, being packed aboard Greene Transfer—they moved me last January 10. Yesterday this same truck loaded all that remains for me to claim from Tuscany Hills Farm. I stop here on my way to 2902 Jefferson Road, the house that will one day feel like home, but right now feels only like a repository of my past homes. This is a low point. I must drive on.

It's midnight now and the movers left about an hour ago. It was a physically exhausting day fraught with moving-related horrors. There were only two men sent to unload what five had loaded. "We can't carry the swing set"; "We can't fit the rolltop desk through that door"; "We can't find the crystal chandelier";

"We don't know how to assemble the bunk beds"—it went on and on. But the swing is where it belongs and the rolltop is where I planned; the bunk beds are indeed assembled and the chandelier was hiding under wrapping blankets in the truck.

There's much to unpack, curtains to hem and hang. I have my work cut out for me, but I expect the place will look just fine when I put in a couple days of labor.

Saturday, August 2

Another physical day. Hours of sorting kids' clothes—ungodly boring. Grocery shopping to fill the cupboards and make the house a home. A surprise visit by Connie and Al Evans on their way somewhere else. Their marriage is deeply troubled—Connie hangs on for fear, Al is strangling—they don't look good at all.

I had a long talk with a strange and attractive man in the next seat at the Waffle House counter. He'd also been to Vietnam and he'd also written about it. Every man is a threat, sexually—every man. I am a walking time bomb, sexually.

Muller—he seems so far away. I feel, really feel that this move to Asheville is a move away from Dave. Damn, I don't want it to be, but it is. The reality of the demands of this new life are so acute, so constant, so physical, so financial and immediate that I can't ignore them. In that way, I guess, this is my step away from the obsession that was David in Watertown.

Perhaps when my life becomes routine again, I will think and ponder in quiet moments about David, but now I cannot. Of course, it may never become routine; there are too many new things at every turn. I'm very tired but sleep isn't so easy these last days here—because I'm so alone in the dark new house.

Friday, August 8

The children returned yesterday from their one-week vacation with Paul in California. Paul's youngest brother was married there and I planned my moving week to coincide with the kids' absence. In these two days, Max, Andrew, and I have been to Max's new school, to the science museum, to the old farmers' market, to a park—all in the heat. The boys are good, good kids. Andrew is consistently easier than Max.

Damn—I just found that my check to the movers bounced. How can I have been $200 off in my checkbook calculations?! I go berserk. Everything feels so hard, everything requires money, everything requires decisions. I have lots of unpleasant dreams and middle-of-the-night awakenings. I even yearn for my marriage when things are so hard.

The Waffle House fellow unexpectedly stops over tonight. He helps me check out my new answering machine. He looks at my red silk roses on the book shelf (a gift last Valentine's Day, from David) and says, "Somebody loves you." I answer, "Somebody used to love me." He says, "We've all had that."

There is so much pressure—pressure to write well, pressure to earn money, pressure to do well by my kids. I cry after the check bounces, and my dear, dear Max comforts me. "Mommy, I know you are sad about the divorce and you still love David." And then he insists I take $4 from his money jar to help me out with the bills. God, that made me cry. I *love* my boys.

Monday, August 18

I have accomplished remarkable things in two and a half weeks here. I've worked, begun group therapy (at Charles Berman's suggestion), cared for the boys for eleven straight days (Paul just took them), found a preschool for Andrew, met and engaged neighbors, chose a new pediatrician, phoned old friends, and was social and charming at two weekend dinner parties. I feel at home here. This town is a good, warm, and welcoming place. A new acquaintance advises me to accept all invitations now—and I do. I seem to be pulling my life together. At the moment, I'm feeling very sexy and even that's a good sign. Every turn I take in Asheville seems to be a good one. It's remarkable.

Wednesday, August 20

I am such a "grown-up." My God, I am such a grown-up, doing all these grown-up things. Me, alone—completely responsible for earning a living, doing a job, caring for two children, keeping a house, paying bills, shopping, cleaning—and all this with no man in sight. Wonderful!!

Last night, I reread all of David's letters and looked at his pictures. I miss him, there's no doubt about that. I want to be held, I want to be loved. I want to give love. But for now, I'm practicing being all grown-up, for the first time in my life, and I'm slowly—very slowly—getting the knack of it.

Friday, August 22

Do I hang onto the idea of David because the alternative is so bleak—no one? Or do I hang on to the idea of David because he is good for me and because I genuinely love him? Does he hang on to the idea of Linda and the kids because the alternative is so frightening—all the unknowns? Is it fair that I occasionally allow myself to think that David is a coward?

Charles Berman has persistently said he worries about the control David exercised in our relationship. He controlled me, Berman said, through his time (he doles it out sparingly) and his money (he buys me what *he* wants me to have). I agree I chose him in reaction to Paul's total lack of control. And I agree that David can want to have things his way, but I maintain that he can also relinquish that control with me and for me.

Berman accuses me of fluctuating between wanting independence and wanting to be cared for. "Sure," I concede, "doesn't everyone?" And he says, "Not to these extremes." He says it relates to my father, who cared for me completely as a child and who I violently rejected in adolescence for a crack at independence. That's been my pattern—extreme vacillation between passive dependence and aggressive independence.

Yes, I want—need—to be independent. That feeling will grow as I continue to do for myself. I'll get used to caring for myself and for the children without daddy or husband. But I also realize that there is a tradeoff if you want to love and be loved—you relinquish some control. And I hope that David can come to realize that, too.

I allow myself to see David's weaknesses and flaws, more and more. And if we were together again, I don't know how it would be for us. I kind of hope it would be better, less intense and treacherous. But who knows? There are doubts, but still I want him now and certainly still I desire him sexually.

All men are sexual objects or threats now. The book *Crazy Time* tells me to listen to my body. My body is saying, loud and clear, "Take it easy and slow, choose wisely when the time is right." My hormones—well, they say "Ye gad, I want a man."

Sunday, August 24

My dear, dear friend of fifteen years flew in from Cleveland to spend forty-eight comforting hours with me. Nothing could have been better for me than Ronnie, *no one*. She and her husband of eighteen years, the friends most exactly like Paul and I, separated last month. I wanted only to cry with her and to hug her. Here, where all is new and rootless, Ronnie brought all these years of history/herstory. I love and need her. This weekend, with a woman I love—and a current story very like my own—is a luxury I've not had before now. Ronnie has had a lot of support from friends, has shared her story with other separated and divorced women. I have not. And now I know that it's harder my way. I guess that's why I've needed to keep this diary.

Tuesday, August 26

It's twenty-four hours after last night's group, and a random comment sparks these thoughts. One group member raved about my "great sense of humor." "You really do laugh at yourself and your problems," he said. I said, "Me?" Then, "In my marriage Paul was the one with the sense of humor, I was defined as humorless." And another group member offered, "Maybe you were so miserable with Paul you couldn't laugh." Was I so oppressed in my marriage that I couldn't laugh? With David I laughed a lot and easily. Lord, am I funny, is that how people see me? The chemistry between David and me was that we were

serious people with *so* much to laugh about. Berman asked me
if David and I would still have been laughing five years down
the road. My goodness, much to think about in this matter of
laughter.

Thursday, August 28

I went out alone to a club tonight for the first time—and the
funniest thing happened. It makes the most terrific story. I wanted
to hear live music, and singer-songwriter Holly Near was per-
forming at this club. But I knew nothing at all about the Asheville
night scene, so I was petrified it would be a meat market and I'd
be put upon. The day before, in the afternoon, I went to the
club, introduced myself to the manager, and asked what sort of
clientele he had. He assured me that it was a most respectable
place and quite all right for "an older single woman."

Still, filled with trepidation and the certainty that I would be
harassed by some unsavory male with gold chains and hairy chest,
I went. Imagine, if you will, my complete amazement when I
walked in, looked at the crowd, and realized that it was 98 percent
female. It turns out Holly Near draws a gay crowd and there were
perhaps 250 coupled women. There was my immediate moment
of realization—and then I simply couldn't stop laughing. My first
night as a woman out alone—my severe paranoid fantasies—
and then, *voila!* all lesbians. Anyway, it was a perfectly lovely
place, terrific music, and a fine evening.

Friday, August 29

I came home tonight, looked in the mirror and found myself
to be a beautiful, beautiful woman. Why am I in such a hurry
to connect with a man?

Monday, September 1

Last night, for the first time, I lay in bed and talked to David's
pictures. I talked honest, beseeching, loving talk. How I wish
that he could hear what it is I say.

I awakened this morning from a dream about Linda Muller:

her hair was cut shoulder-length, colored a chestnut brown, and permed at the ends. She looked terrific and she looked happy. And for the first time I wondered, is it possible that she and he are happy? Is it possible that she is transforming—looking good, looking for work, responding to her husband? That possibility has *never* before occurred to me. I've always assumed that he hangs on to a miserable marriage, but when I awakened from my dream this morning, I wasn't so sure and I felt guilty for wanting Linda's husband.

But I *am* lonely—lonely for good conversation, good loving, good sex, good shared ideas.

Asheville—it's only been one month today—a more than adequate and busy first month.

Tuesday, September 2

First day of school thoughts: I felt enormous anxiety for my children beginning their new schools, but they seemed to do very well. Do we ever really know? The schools are lovely, but the mothers! "She doesn't *have* to work," is the phrase these women of the neighborhood repeat about one another. It's a fact they're proud of—of being supported by hard-working men. It never crosses their minds that there could be another point to working. It's a boast that my mother used to make forty years ago, but in this day and age, it seems very odd. These women are insulated by their Southernness and their affluence—very unworldly.

Wednesday, September 3

It's the second day of school and Andrew looked serious and contemplative, alone in line for school. Max looked scared as he hurried his good-bye and ran into his school. He cries at school that he misses his father. With the beginning of school, we're on the new schedule—Paul has the boys from Friday at five P.M. until Sunday at six P.M. and during most school vacations. Max already equates the brevity of visits to his father with the beginning of first grade.

I'm feeling very unsettled right now, very uncertain. Things do not feel easy—this balancing of kids, work, self—so many women do it and now I do, too. The isolation of my work is no great asset, either. Keep plugging, Inette, Berman says it *will* get better (psychotherapeutic litany).

Saturday, September 6

Increasingly in Asheville, I'm boosted and accepted as this important New York writer. I'm asked to be the speaker at the synagogue's annual fundraiser—to talk about my experiences as a correspondent in Vietnam—and it's very validating. I'm invited by a lovely couple to the local symphony board's black-tie event at a Southern gentleman's club—very posh and socially important. If I decided methodically to take social Asheville by storm, it appears I could. This week I'll meet the executive editor of the newspaper, the station manager at several television stations, the local magazine editor. So I move to this social neighborhood, cultivate certain people on the strength of this writer identity, and I haven't yet seen dollar one from writing here. In my bum moments, I think I'm a phony—all bluff and presentation.

Damn, it's been a hell of a week—all the emotions of getting the kids settled in school, the guilts, and the lack of time. I bake cupcakes for Max's birthday party at school, I put together a half-dozen GI Joe abominations for his birthday, I worry about money. I need to be affirmed by work, and this freelance process does take time—patience in the face of dwindling resources is tough. I need a credit card badly, and I get refused for some obscure reason. There are serious pressures and I'm trying to appear so together and hot shit, and it feels very schizoid.

Saturday, September 13

What I wish to say here is that I'm only just today having my first fleeting insight into the magnitude of what I've done. Always, always until now, I've been so emotionally charged by the moment I was living that I could see and feel only that moment.

But today, at some point—like an epiphany—the whole passed quickly before my eyes, and I'm just overwhelmed by what I've done this past year. It is mammoth.

A part of me wishes I could love, respect, and desire Paul. The boys always speak of him with great warmth—and it would make my life so easy. Paul is sweet, considerate, generous, honest, unpretentious, and I value him so much. But I'm not attracted to him and I guess I don't love him enough. Another part of me knows that I've in no way relinquished my hope for David. Still I believe he's bright, sensitive, full of ideas, ambitious—he laughs and cries with me. He isn't perfect—oh, no, not perfect—but wonderful, nonetheless. And despite, in some ways, wishing that I did not—I love him.

Friday, September 19

A couple—neighbors of Paul's and mine from the farm—visited me in Asheville tonight and took me out to dinner. They presented several versions of the Watertown opinion of David. "Why did you put us through all of this if it wasn't really love?" was one accusation. "Because he returned to his wife, it must have been a tawdry affair—he must have just needed to bed someone," was another. Or, "His marriage wasn't that bad after all." Finally, "He didn't want to give up his good practice and his money."

I feel so weird that, in all of this, everyone—absolutely everyone—except me, sees the relationship with David as over. Of course, it *has* been five months since he left the apartment.

Saturday, September 20

I'm very sad right now. I've had the kids for two solid weeks without break, and they've just left so I guess I'm due a collapse. It would be very nice to have a boyfriend. It would be very nice to have a regular date and regular affection from an adult male. In fact, it would be nice to have an understanding woman friend who's in the same place I am. I guess for all the talking I do, all the social conversation I make, I'm very alone and very lonely.

Sunday, September 28

Max talks constantly about his alternate weekends with Paul's girlfriend Peggy. He tells me what a "fine woman" this Peggy is—how she buys him toys, how she hugs daddy. And I feel jealousy. But I'm fairly certain that I'm jealous not of Paul, but of his having a relationship when I do not. I also admit to feeling pangs of envy for this other woman in my children's lives. Yet I am grateful this woman is kind and generous to my boys. I get flashes of this woman sleeping in what was once my bed—that huge canopy bed. But then David lay in that bed too—quite a bed!

Monday, September 29

I think, perhaps, I've turned a corner. I no longer believe— really believe—that if I wait long enough, David will return and we'll live happily ever after. I reread the segment of this journal from February until May and some things are revealed to me. (1) I looked foolish hanging on after David left me. I was foolish not to listen to David's own words and doubts. I looked pathetic clinging to something other than the writing on the wall. (2) The months that I lived with him were crazy—high stress, high doubt on my part, absolutely crazy. It was not the best situation in which to decide with whom to spend the rest of my life.

Maybe I've been clinging to shadows and refusing the truth that everyone saw but me. These new insights scare me. I will now truly be alone. I'm sure that this doesn't end my fantasies for good and all, but tonight I do not want to put myself to sleep looking at David's pictures and rereading his letters.

This diary—whatever other purpose it serves—has always been truthful. I've never fudged on the truth as I felt it at the time. So now I allow the diary to shine some light, and those two truths I've recorded here are rather glaring. I still don't want to be alone.

Wednesday, October 1

Charles Berman said today that I'm not yet ready to have a relationship with a new man who may combine the best qualities of Paul and David—but that will come in time. He congratulated me on this time in Asheville, this time alone. "You would never have freed yourself from Paul if you had remained with David. You'll now know that you worked it all out, the whole process—that you gave it your best shot." I'm gradually making progress.

Thursday, October 2

It's evening, my sons are asleep, the air conditioner hums and cools in this October heat. I've been pleasurably reading from Mary Gordon's *Men and Angels,* and she speaks to me. I just walked into my study—dark except for the stained glass desk lamp—and I think how much I love this room, perhaps more than any one room I've ever lived in. Maybe that's simply because it reflects my independence right now. No one is directing me but me, no one is making decisions for my life but me. It's a really wonderful room: knotty pine walls, my oak rolltop desk, my books, my signed Hemingway photos, my new James Dean poster, and me. I also love my bedroom—again, maybe because it's completly mine. It's hard to picture a man in it except completely on my terms, and I still have no idea what those terms may be. I also enjoy this living room, filled with some of my favorite things from different places and times in my life. Anyway, tonight in this 1955 rambler, I am enjoying my home. This is a comfortable place, I feel safe in this house.

It's October, and last October my fantasies of D.M. were overtaking me. *Ahhh*—that wonderful sensation of falling in love. "The narcotic of romantic love," Berman likes to say. *Mmmmm* . . .

Friday, October 3

It is proper that my writing work should go hard, should be rough getting started. I've always looked for quick fixes, but I cannot do that anymore. I undersand that I must work, sweat, cry, and agonize for what I want—for what is worth having: my children, my financial independence, my self-esteem, a good relationship with a worthy man. I feel so decent right now—so human, so adult, so ready to face the consequences. My God, this has not been a bad year at all.

Saturday, October 4

I just finished Mary Gordon's book and I want to cry. "Perhaps," she said, "that was what made the different between adults and children. Adults knew they were alone; their solitude was final, and there was no rescue."

And also: " 'For privacy,' she felt, 'was one of the important benefits of marriage. It was much easier to have privacy in a marriage than as a single woman; there was a time for it, and time to come back out of it, a place to come back to . . . it didn't bring the house down.' "

Sunday, October 5

It is this week between Rosh Hashana (the Jewish New Year) and Yom Kippur when we are to ask forgiveness of those we have wronged in the year past. This is a very spiritual and serious time for me. I have always done some good thinking at this time. In the spirit of starting the New Year soundly, I've written to Paul. These are parts of the letter.

Dear Paul,

I ask you to forgive me the hurts I have inflicted on you and on our sons. There is no matter of deserving or not deserving. I can't say I would do this year differently—could, in fact, have done it differently—or even that I'd want to.

But I expect that, because of this year, I am not as innocent and incognizant as I was a year ago. Perhaps I am not as irresponsible. Certainly I am no longer a believer in certainty and perfection.

I think I'm finally becoming a grown-up. I can't begin to predict what follows from that for my future . . .

I wish you l'shana tova—a very good year.

Inette

Tuesday, October 7

This was a beautiful autumnal day, and with Andrew napping in the car, I headed out through the countryside for a few hours. I'd forgotten the extraordinary beauty of the mountains and the country. How could I have forgotten? I felt as though I had this physical need of it—a need to feel those open spaces, that green, that topography—and when I returned to Asheville, I felt very hemmed in by the city.

On the drive, I thought a lot about David, and I could actually feel him loosening his hold on me. It will be six months tomorrow since he left the apartment we shared. I simply do not trust my memory anymore. I don't know the reality of David and me. More and more I think he'll call and ask, "Do you still love me?" and I'd have to say, "I don't know." It is getting to be a long time and the accuracy of my memory is no longer reliable. What was there? What is there?

I'm neither helpless nor needy. I'm feeling good, loving my boys like crazy, liking this little house and this little city, and feeling comfortable.

Wednesday, October 8

I've just returned from a pivotal session with Charles Berman. I'm finally letting go of David. I just took the basket of his photographs and letters and moved it away from the side of my bed, up into the recesses of the attic.

The pity is that I'll never know what David and I may have become. The marvelous thing is that I'll never know what we may have become. Pick your poison.

Charles Berman said, "You may feel that you've given up a lot this year, but you have grown and changed."

David, I am letting go. I have held on so tenaciously for so long. I am letting go. There were many, many tears at Charles Berman's today; many, many tears.

Sunday, October 19

I just saw off my mother and father at the airport—they've been visiting for four days. It was a very good visit. My father was wonderful: kind, warm, loving. The first night here, after dinner, he spoke to me in a way that he never has. He described his tough times as a young man, about feeling down and feeling beaten. "But, Inette," he said, "life does turn around—it doesn't set out to keep kicking you over and over." He spoke in a tone and a way that I've never before heard from my father. He is a fine man. I've lost a lot in relinquishing the man who is my father over the years, in refusing to allow each of us to know the other.

This visit I was pretty straight with both of them. I tried to break through the old patterns of trying to please. I talked about my pain, about what is difficult in my life. I asked my mother to listen, not advise. I told her to listen and then tell me that she understands. And at times, I was successful. In a funny way, it's easier without Paul—I didn't have to feel the slights on his behalf.

My mother, very typically, said that my diary should end when "you get a big job—when you're successful." She also said, typically, so-and-so is "brilliant [because] he makes millions"; or "He's successful and talented because he makes big money." Her idea of brilliance and success and talent are so circumscribed—they reflect the values of her generation. It's hard to separate what she wants for me from what I want for myself.

But I will give both my parents their due. They are caring and they feel my pain. They realize what I'm doing here and how hard it is. God, parents, and children—my parents and me, my children and me.

It was a very good visit, but I do have to be on my toes for my defensiveness, my reactions to them. God, therapy is wonderful. What would therapy have done for my mother?

Monday, October 20

My father left a check on my desk for $500. This, despite my constant expressed wish that he give me *no* money at this time. I'm reading *The Cinderella Complex* about women and their dependency on men. I put that check in an envelope and sent it back to my father. I'm broke and it was very hard to do, but I feel wonderful!

Tuesday, October 21

I am on my way—moving toward self-sufficiency for the first time. It is a process. Will I want David when I'm there? Will I want Paul? Will I be content to be alone? I really don't know.

I look at the little airplanes in the sky, and I still, seven years after my first flying lesson, yearn to be flying them. I yearn to be up there in that sparkling, clear, blue sky. Will I? The fun is knowing I can do it—and I will pay for it myself.

Thursday, October 23

Today is one year since the first time I climbed in bed with David Muller, and I suppose absolutely nothing will happen to commemorate that day. But know that I'm dying to call him, to write him, to send him a telegram—for that matter I'm dying to kiss him, to touch him, to fuck him. I feel the power of this anniversary, the power of his thoughts mingling right now with mine, the power of my wishful thinking. But I won't call.

I am not angry at David. I guess I never really have been. We are only humans, fumbling along trying to do the right thing for ourselves and for a few others. But how long can I continue to believe that he loves me? How long can I indulge myself in these pipe dreams? Do I need to indulge myself in order to get through these months? Is it all part of the process? I will make it without David, and I won't cling to Paul for lack of Dave. I will make it alone, and someday when I am strong in my aloneness, I will form a good, solid, healthy, passion-filled relationship with another man. I will love again and it will be from strength. These are not just words. Maybe someday I will look at David Muller and say he was not the one—but now I must confess that I'd give the world to have that choice, that chance.

I reread the journal from last autumn and I fall in love all over again. I read my journal from last December—the conflict, the confusion, the pain—and I no longer wish to call David. I cannot head back to that stuff in any form. He and I were just plunging into the affair and then living together to silence the uncertainties. I can't do it like that again. Future moves will be more considered, more reasoned. Now I must wait, wait and live, live my life and wait. Who can predict the future? Not a single soul. Not the shrinks, not the actors, no one. We just live it day by day.

This particular day has every right to be difficult—it has every right to extract some suffering.

Sunday, October 26

I knew, even as I walked out of Dr. Charles Berman's office two days ago, that this was the session during which my shrink earned his nine months of psychiatric fees. Of course, it's all cumulative—there is no one pivotal moment in therapy that happens independent of all that preceded it. But today was consequential.

Berman was confrontational, and that's not his usual tack. Obviously, this man knows me very well, has his finger on my pulse, and knew exactly what I needed now—what I was ready to hear.

It was the day after the one-year anniversary of that life-changing date at the Country Inn. I described to Berman that I'd spent the anniversary day rereading my journal—remembering, forgetting, spanning the whole range of my feelings. After which I blurted, "Well, now there remains only David's fortieth birthday on December 16 to commemorate—the very last time I have a legitimate reason to write him."

And Berman looked me in the face and said, "Why? What do you hope to accomplish?" Then, rather angrily, he said, "Sure you can think about doing that, if it helps you get through the next three months!" He proceeded to lecture me about self-esteem, about how "some women who allow themselves to be vulnerable and come out feeling rejected, some women . . ." He said, "You laid down your rules, Inette, and it's important for your self-esteem to stick to them."

I left the session feeling angry at Berman. I left with a vague sense of anxiety and frustration and a specific sense of anger. But like all good therapy, the kind that counts for something seeps into your pores and gradually passes into your nervous system—until days, weeks, or months later you realize what it was you heard and what that means.

Within forty-eight hours, I knew that I was not one of those women who allow themselves to feel like shit. I knew for the first time—*knew*—that I would never again initiate contact with David Muller, that my last letter had said it all.

The reason that I cannot reach out to David is that I must be able to make demands of him. *He* has to come to *me* or not come at all—so that I can say to him, "I want more of your time" (we'd often discussed alternatives to a two-man practice); "I want us to respect each other's independence"; "I don't want to control you, but I don't want to be controlled by you, either"; "I want to love you and be loved by you."

I know I will never contact Muller. There's no point. Why live a fantasy? Why hang on for crumbs? I'm worth a whole lot more than that. I expect that I'll be alone for a while before I'm ready to form another relationship. I better settle into my work and my kids, maybe make some real, new friendships.

I drive around and I think, "I have booted David Muller out of my life for the first time." I can feel, inside of me, the difference since last Friday's therapy. Just two weeks ago, I moved the basket of David memorabilia away from my bed—now I've actually moved Dave himself. There's no more *trying* to keep that fire alive. What's in it for me?

My most spiritual friend Wendy echoed my sentiments with her words, "It is not that you love him less. It's just that there's less attachment. It has a sad side, of course, because at least while you're in there fighting, you believe you can manipulate someone else's process. But now you are saying, 'I give it over to the universe.' "

So I have decided that I no longer want to make myself think of him and keep the faith and wait for him to return and influence his return. Rather, I want to be sane and sensible and rational and accept that it's over. It's pointless and unhealthy to hang on. I guess my brother was right that I will never forget David Muller, and I can live with that, too. I will never forget him, and in some inconsequential way, I may always love him, but he can no longer be allowed to block my other avenues, whatever they may be.

Anyway, last Friday was a critical turning point. Perhaps I gave up something in deciding to let go of David, but it feels much more like I redeemed something of myself.

Monday, October 27

I slept in until 8:30 this morning and awakened from a wonderfully sensual, emotionally satisfying dream of making love to Ted Kennedy (and I always thought it was John whom I'd choose). The senator and I were wandering through some old and very urban setting (Boston? New York?). I wanted so badly to go back to sleep and return to the love making because this was the first time I've dreamed of screwing someone other than David or Paul—and it felt very healthy.

Tuesday, October 28

A variety of people have been describing me in most flattering ways lately. They've said, when introducing me to still other new people, that I'm "bright," "funny," "dynamic," "a great storyteller." Maybe I am those things, but I'm not yet crazy about myself. I still think at times that I'm a phony. Yet I know that I'm at my best these days because I'm at my most vulnerable—

laughing at my own foibles—instead of entrenched in my old position of defensiveness. I would love to go out dancing right now.

Wednesday, October 29

Significantly, I believe, I drove to the Hillsdale Psychiatric Hospital and parked out on the street in front for ten minutes. This is the first time I've gone anywhere near that place in the five months since I've left it. My goodness, time does pass. I just sat in my car—outside the parking lot because I was afraid to get closer—stared at the building, and tried to visualize the interior floor plan and myself inside it. I looked at that place and listened to the music on my tape player, and it seemed very scary indeed to be a patient locked inside that hospital. I've come a very great distance in this time. My God, I was actually a patient in a psychiatric hospital—it's amazing! It's even more amazing that I remember *loving* that hospital. Charles Berman was right—it wasn't the place that was so wonderful, I simply used that place, "used it up," got what could be gotten from it. The credit is mine.

Thursday, October 30

In the midst of my work, I look at my face in the mirror. It is softening, kind of rounding with age, but that's not so bad. I look at the face of the young college graduate in mortarboard on my office wall and the other photograph of the twenty-three-year-old me in combat fatigues. It feels as though I lived then, but then I ceased to live for a period of time—and now I live again. I feel very alive and very growing and that is wonderful. But the measure of my aliveness is no longer calculated in flashes and splashes and glitter and show, as it was in those early years. No, ma'am; it's now far more internal.

Yesterday I had a conversation with my mother. "People have been describing me as a 'good storyteller,' " I said. "I guess, I'm changing." She responded, "Becoming more extroverted and outgoing." "No," I said, "not that. Rather I'm more willing to

expose the parts of me that I've always repressed and hidden."
She was disappointed. "Oh . . ." is what she said.

Sunday, November 2

Everything continues to be tough, everything feels like a crisis
to be dealt with. I begin to understand the idea of yin and yang.
Every good thing has a not-so-good counterforce, every contest
won is a debt owed, every accomplishment will extract a toll.
You cannot have lived forty years and not understand that. My
belief in "perfect moments" is a belief that only the very young
can afford to hang on to.

Things are tough for me because I have exposed myself this
year, been vulnerable, as I've never been before. In a sense, I've
ripped up all the givens. And operating without them means
everything has to be redefined in every situation.

It's a beautiful fall day—the very last of them—the leaves are
falling fast. And as the Rolling Stones recorded in 1969 and the
movie *The Big Chill* replayed, "You can't always get what you
want, but if you try sometime, you might find, you get what you
need."

Saturday, November 29

I've spent the past three days walking the wooded trails of the
Blue Ridge Parkway with my friend of eighteen years, Emily.
This woman was a colleague at my very first newspaper job and
the only nonfamily guest at my tiny wedding. We walked fifteen
miles at a stretch. We slogged through wet leaves and mud
puddles. We talked. At the time, we stepped out, hopped boul-
ders and fallen branches without keeping track of either time or
miles—and the words flowed. It was a cleansing three days. Only
now do I feel the extreme muscular pain in my calves and nighttime cramps.

Emily and I hadn't seen one another for three years, not since
I was pregnant with Andrew. This was the first time we'd allowed
more than a year to pass between visits. This year, we've spoken
a great deal by phone and, throughout my crises, Emily has been

her usual loyal, caring, restrained, and calm self. In our relationship, I've been the risk taker and she's been the stable one. She's forty-one now and has been through a hell of a couple years herself—serious emotional problems with her teenage daughter. I never, in our walks and talks, felt like I was dumping on Emily. It was much more that we were sharing—sharing our toughest years and the rock bottom of our feelings. Emily is not one who opens up easily, so it is very flattering when it happens.

Again, as during Ronnie's visit last September, I had that wonderful feeling of touching roots—of cozily settling into the comfort and understanding of an old friendship. I can only say that, as a result, my head feels clear and I am emotionally purged.

But I write now at length because there's been a genuine revelation—it appears they are coming fast and furious these days. Throughout the course of our walks, I found myself talking about my marriage—about the assumptions implicit in the marriage. For the duration of the marriage Paul has consistently defined me in a variety of negative ways and I have never for a moment doubted the validity of his assessments. So he has said, and ultimately I say about myself, that I am humorless, sexually unadventurous, not a very original thinker, not an intellectual, closed to all new possibilities, and a babbler. Paul, by implication, is the opposite—he holds the high ground in all categories. He said, and finally I believed with all my heart, that I'm not much of a writer, my style of dress is boring, my social ease is phony, my lavish entertaining is compulsive. Paul never complimented me, he never told me there was a thing he liked about me, and he never volunteered that he loved me until after he knew of the affair. Still, Paul starts all his sentences to me with, "You always . . ." or "You never . . ."

For the first time, in the course of the miles of walk and the hours of talk with Emily, I questioned the validity of Paul's consistently unflattering assessment of me. I would say to Emily, "I'm boring." She would answer, "Inette, you're electric." I'd say, "I'm plodding, afraid of change." She'd answer, "You are the most adventurous person I know." I'd say, "I'm selfish." She'd answer, "You're emotionally very generous." And in this way, over three days, the pattern emerged. *"Shit,"* I finally screamed. *"Shit, shit, shit*—he is dead wrong—I *am* adventurous, electric, I'm not the least bit selfish."

Look, I know that no one can make me love myself or prevent me from loving myself. But damn, I've bought into this stuff in a major way. All my best qualities became negatives over the years. My mother, although she was always there for me, told me in a million spoken and unspoken ways that I wasn't worth much and Paul picked up the slack where she left off. I replicated the relationship with my mother. In public and private, I would laugh at Paul's humorous putdowns—it was our shared joke that "Inette is a bitch." When I told Emily for the ten-thousandth time that "Paul is the funny one," she could restrain herself no longer. "Inette, there is nothing at all funny about demeaning your wife in public—that is *not* funny."

I'm acutely aware that the unspoken assumption of this marriage has always been that Paul was the fragile one, that his ego needed building—and since I was the strong one (the competent one), that was my job. I, it was agreed, was the arrogant one and Paul's job was to take me down a peg or two. My self-image was defined by Paul and I accepted his definition as gospel. I was his booster and his loyal advocate. He was the man who would puncture my inflated balloon. But that balloon was filled with hot air—I never genuinely loved myself—and so this man that I loved made me feel like shit (rather, confirmed what I already believed). Emily profoundly asked, "Does Paul label you to contain you—to counter his own insecurity when he confronts you? Does he put you down to elevate himself?"

I have a very poigant memory here from the last year I lived with Paul. Paul had a business lunch with a professional writer out of New York and another woman of my acquaintance. After the lunch, this woman called to tell me (somewhat jealously) that Paul had spent the entire meal bragging about "my wife, the writer." She said that he visibly glowed with pride and persisted in listing my accomplishments. Like a sharply focused photograph, I can even now remember my feeling when I heard this—amazement. My mouth fell open, I could not believe it! I could not believe that Paul *felt* these wonderful things about me. I mentioned the exchange to Paul, along with my reaction, and he just smiled sweetly at me. I was so touched, so moved, so loved. It was a very special moment. I have never, except in the early years of our relationship and immediately after the birth of our first child, felt admired by the man I loved.

It is no wonder, then, that I have been addicted to David Muller—he loved everything about me and he *told* me. He loved the things I already was, I didn't have to change to be loved. He believed, and convinced *me* that he believed, that the way I look is beautiful—my body, just as it is, is perfect; that my conversation is enlightened and entertaining; my worldliness is titillating; my sexuality was the answer to his deepest fantasies. It was very heady stuff for someone who never heard such words. No wonder I cannot easily relinquish David Muller. No wonder I have felt so much unexpressed anger at Paul.

My God, the pieces of the Hillsdale puzzle now fall into place: my rage in Terry's psychodrama; the group telling me that all of Paul's fine qualities were "not enough" for me; my lack of assertiveness—I have not made demands of Paul; my glaring lack of self-love and my mother's contribution to that.

Paul's motives were clear. Denigrating me was the way he built his self-esteem. Not only was he attracted to a strong woman because it meant he came to share that power but he was also able to increase his own self-worth by diminishing mine. It has taken me one full year to understand this point. I've tenaciously refused to understand it for some self-protective but also self-defeating reason. My refusal was self-protective because it allowed me to hang on to the marriage. Now, when I reread the Hillsdale Psychiatric Hospital journal, it takes on real meaning. I finally understand. Let it be said here that letting go of this marriage is the godawful hardest thing that this woman can do.

So here I am in Asheville, with some money from magazine work, the beginning of a career, my sons, an active social life, and a great deal of personal satisfaction in taking care of myself. I'm liking myself better than I have in ages, perhaps ever. I'm feeling hopeful about my future. And yet, yet, yet—I've not wanted to let go of this marriage. Perhaps it's a simple case of the known always being preferable to the unknown. Perhaps it's my bedrock belief that marriage is forever. Perhaps it's a case of genuinely liking an awful lot of things about Paul. Perhaps it's the point that Charles Berman makes: "Your spoken contract may have been that Paul disapproved of you, but the unspoken contract has always been that he adored you—loves you still."

But walking these last days through the woods along the Blue Ridge Parkway with a friend of eighteen years, I've finally allowed myself to understand that the price I paid for Paul's love was too great. I believe I'm now ready for the divorce.

Thursday, December 4

This diary is going to end here. It's not going to end as it began—with a concrete event, titillation—the big bang. It won't end with me dressed in semiwhite at the altar of matrimony, and it won't end with me in a navy blue business suit at the divorce court. There will be no descent of a 120 piece orchestra. This diary ends today because I've sold it for publication as a book—and that effectively ends it. There are eyes reading over my shoulder now and I become self-conscious. There is an audience, and my writing reacts to that—the spontaneity and honesty of the journal are gone.

I'm satisfied that, in fact, this journal can't really end. The act of opening doors—prodded by this midlife search—doesn't end. That's too facile. Therapy continues and my therapist assures me that another six months will write its own insights. And in point of fact, why should the reader—my God, now there *is* a reader—know more than I can know about the future?

Friday, December 5

I feel compelled to write one last entry here. My circle of friends has grown in recent weeks to include a number of single women. Each is around my age, and most are newly abandoned by a husband of some duration. Others have done the abandoning. I recognize their despair, their fears, and their hopelessness. I want to say to them—and I sometimes do—"Don't fight it, don't be afraid." But I'm not sure it helps.

Midlife crisis is not a bad joke. Midlife is, I believe, an unequaled opportunity for change and growth—and God knows there aren't a whole lot of those in our lives. Our lives usually follow form. Generally we are locked in by jobs, by children, by tradition, by family expectation, by neighbors' patterns of behavior—and we work very hard to keep things the same, to keep things on track.

Of course, in adolescence all that breaks loose and perhaps during other times as well—but not often. Most assuredly, in midlife we are offered one of life's unique chances to shake the status quo—to explore our personal possibilities.

But change is always always painful. Divorce is never not agonizing. Examination of the things we have always taken for granted is remarkably disorienting and frightening. And it is impossible immediately to substitute one neat set of ideas and one regime for another. Into the opening surge all the confusing possibilities.

I did not behave here with gentility and grace, kindness and elegance. This diary is in many, many places acutely embarrassing. I behaved erratically, inconsistently, and irrationally. But I believed there lurked a certain underlying rationality that my gut—that place that often leads you into the storm but seldom into the grave—dictated. I'm glad that I allowed my gut free reign—no, I did not *allow* it—but I'm glad it happened.

My life will again settle down to patterns and systems. It probably already has. But because of my thirty-ninth and fortieth years and the way I lived them, I am forever changed and how *can* I regret that?